THE TROJAN WAR

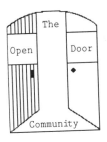

BOOKS BY
Olivia E. Coolidge

GREEK MYTHS
LEGENDS OF THE NORTH
THE TROJAN WAR

THE
TROJAN
WAR

By Olivia E. Coolidge

ILLUSTRATED BY

Edouard Sandoz

HOUGHTON MIFFLIN COMPANY · BOSTON

Printed in the United States of America

HC ISBN 0-395-06731-6
PA ISBN 0-395-56151-5

AGM 10 9 8 7 6 5 4 3 2 1

CONTENTS

A TABLE OF
The Chief Characters

GODS

ZEUS	King of gods and men.
HERA	Wife of Zeus, a chief supporter of the Greeks.
POSEIDON	God of the sea, a supporter of the Greeks.
ATHENE	Goddess of wisdom, a chief supporter of the Greeks.
APHRODITE	Goddess of beauty, chief supporter of the Trojans.
APOLLO	God of the sun, a supporter of the Trojans.
THETIS	A sea goddess, mother of Achilles.

GREEKS

AGAMEMNON	Overlord of Greece.
CLYTEMNESTRA	His wife.
MENELAUS	His brother.
HELEN	Menelaus' wife.
ACHILLES	Greatest of the heroes.

PYRRHUS   His son.

ODYSSEUS   Wisest of the heroes.

PENELOPE   His wife.

AJAX   Son of Telamon, an immensely strong,
                   but stupid hero.

AJAX   Son of Oileus, a swift runner.

DIOMEDE   Companion to Odysseus on several ad-
                   ventures.

NESTOR   Oldest of the heroes.

TROJANS

PRIAM   King of Troy.

HECUBA   His wife.

HECTOR   His bravest son.

PARIS   His most beautiful son.

CASSANDRA   His daughter, a prophetess.

HELENUS   Twin brother of Cassandra, a prophet.

DEIPHOBUS   A son of Priam, third husband of Helen.

ANDROMACHE   Wife of Hector.

ANTENOR   An old counselor and leader of the
                   peace party.

AENEAS   A son of Aphrodite and second cousin
                   of the princes by his father. Destined
                   to survive the sack of Troy and found
                   a new nation.

INTRODUCTION

For the greater part of three thousand years since the date of the Trojan War, the imagination of poets and dramatists has been busy with its story. This has become the subject of the most famous of all legends and has inspired many of the greatest works of literature that the world has produced. For this reason parts of the tale are very familiar, yet because of the length of the whole, the connection between one well-known episode and another is often obscure. The *Iliad* begins in the tenth year of a war whose origin and ending it does not explain. Shakespeare's *Troilus and Cressida,* Goethe's *Iphigenie,* and Racine's *Andromaque* are concerned with isolated incidents that introduce heroes about whom a great deal more needs to be known.

No author of great merit has attempted to deal with the legend of the Trojan War as a whole. The task has been left to minor poets and compilers of summaries, most of whom are imperfectly acquainted with the details of the story or do not understand the customs of the time about which they write.

The characters of heroes have been changed, or absurd incidents have been invented to fill out gaps in the legend. This in turn has made it more difficult for later generations to gain a complete picture of the story.

In spite of these difficulties, the tale of the Trojan War is one that can and should be told. When a few absurdities are omitted, the legend is surprisingly coherent, in spite of its length and the immense time it has taken to grow. When we read it as a whole, we realize that it is a favorite legend because it is an unusually good one. Its heroes are lifelike people with whom we can sympathize. The story itself is varied, exciting, pathetic, and beautiful all at once. Not to know it is to miss a real pleasure. For its own sake, and not merely as a background to our reading, we can enjoy the story of the Trojan War.

THE
TROJAN
WAR

PART 1

PROLOGUE

1

The Golden Apple

THREE great urns stood by the threshold of Zeus, who was ruler of gods and men. One was filled with the blessings he showered on mortals, but two contained sorrows, for the lives of the heroes were tragic, though glorious in war. War, like all human fortune, came to men from the gods. The most famous of struggles, that between the Greeks and the Trojans, had its origin in the home of the immortals on the mountain peaks of Olympus. There the source of the quarrel can be traced back to the moment when Allfather Zeus caught sight of Thetis, the sea nymph, racing over the sparkling waves with the wind behind her.

Zeus wooed silver-footed Thetis and would have made her his bride, though she was as hard to catch as the sun on the dancing water. It seemed, however, that a curious prophecy was rumored about her: she should have a son who would be greater than his father. When Zeus·heard this tale, he no longer desired the goddess, perceiving that his own rule must be ended if a god became greater than he. Indeed, to make all sure, he determined to wed Thetis to a mortal, that her son might be glorious only among men.

Peleus, king of the Myrmidons, was the chosen bridegroom. Zeus taught him how to seize the goddess as she was playing in the ripples off the shore, and how to hold her fast. Although the angry nymph changed to fire, water, wind, sea gull, tiger, lion, serpent, and finally cuttlefish to escape him, Peleus would not let her go until she had promised to be his bride. Then Zeus, since he had his way, held a stately marriage feast for Thetis and Peleus, to which the gods were bidden.

Few mortals have been done such honor as Peleus when the gods and goddesses sat down to feast with him. Their drink was nectar and their food strange and sweet-smelling. They were dazzling in their loveliness, gay in their laughter. The unwilling bride sat silent by Peleus, but the others were merry, and music such as men can but dream of arose in their midst. They were at harmony one with another, for the evil goddess, dark Discord, was not among them. She alone had not been invited and sat in the empty halls of Olympus, brooding over revenge. Therefore, when the feast was at its height, Discord appeared in a flash and stood scowling at the board. She threw something on the table and vanished without a word to the astonished gods.

It was a golden apple, a rare treasure, around which ran

an inscription, "For the Fairest." In a moment all was clamor as each of the goddesses stretched forth her hand. There was stately Hera, queen of the gods, gray-eyed Athene, golden Aphrodite, and noble Demeter, whose hair was the color of ripe corn. Pretty, rosy Hebe, Artemis, the radiant moon huntress, the slender Graces — each in her own fashion was beautiful beyond compare. Each made her claim for the apple, and the gods joined in the wrangle, supporting this one or that.

Soon the tables were deserted and the bride and groom forgotten, but still in the divine halls of Olympus the endless dispute went on. Even Zeus could do nothing to stop it, for his own wife, Hera, was among the foremost claimants. Years went by, and many goddesses were rejected, but between Hera, Athene, and Aphrodite the gods could make no decision. It was hard to judge between splendor, wisdom, and woman's loveliness, since each has a beauty all its own. Finally, in weariness all agreed that an impartial judge should settle the contest. They would choose a man, youthful and ignorant, who knew none of the goddesses, and let him decide. For this purpose they turned to Mount Ida, where Paris, a young shepherd, kept his flocks on slopes overlooking the high stone walls that surrounded the city of Troy.

Long years before, while the golden apple still ripened in the garden of the gods, Queen Hecuba had awakened on a windy morning and sent messengers running through the streets of Troy to summon the soothsayers. She had dreamed that the son she hoped to bear was no child, but a flaming torch. Fire had spread from it through the doorways of the palace, out into the wide streets, across to the temples, until the very walls of the city were washed in a sea of flame. As the queen opened her eyes, the crash of falling buildings and the shrieks of women were ringing in her frightened ears.

The soothsayers listened gravely to the story of the queen, and with one voice they declared that this dream was a warning of evil. The boy to be born would cause destruction to the city and everything therein.

"That he shall never do," said King Priam grimly. "Have I not other children, and did not you soothsayers prophesy that I should have in all no less than fifty sons? What is the life of one child against the welfare of all? Take him up into the wilds of Mount Ida and leave him there to die."

The king's word was duly obeyed, but a few poor shepherds who roamed in the wilderness found the child and had pity on it, for it was as beautiful as a star. Paris, or Alexandros, grew up within sight of his father's city, knowing nothing of his birth.

Paris tended his sheep on Mount Ida and was happy there, because his nature was soft and peaceful and he was ignorant of the world. Nor was his life hard, for a nymph, Oenone, fell in love with his golden curls and ruddy cheeks burned brown by the open air. Every movement he made was graceful; his voice was low and deep; he shone with such beauty that he seemed a fitting bridegroom even for a goddess. Therefore Oenone wooed Paris and won him, and the two lived together in happiness far from the homes of gods or men.

For his very innocence of mind the gods now chose Paris

to judge between them. They sent him the apple, and the three goddesses appeared to him in a glade, bidding him decide which was the most fair.

The simple shepherd of Mount Ida was stunned by the heavenly beauty of the fairest goddesses. Sunlight flooded their white shoulders and gleamed on their golden hair. The grass broke forth into flowers wherever they pressed their feet. He forgot the wind in the trees around him, the cry of his lambs, and even the cold apple clutched in his hand. The presence of the goddesses brought visions of distant palaces, of minstrels in royal halls singing of heavenly wisdom, of the faces of listening princesses of wonderful beauty. His thoughts were far away amid things he had never seen and scarcely heard of, and among which he was quite unfitted to judge.

Then stepped forth the stately Hera, queen of queens, while he gaped at her from her flashing crown to the purple crocus flowers that stood stiffly round her feet.

"I will make you the king of the world," she said proudly to him and stood waiting while gold thrones, gorgeous processions, and battles, terrifying and distant, chased through the shepherd's simple mind. He made no answer to Hera, since he was stunned by her, but he stood in awed silence, staring until the proud goddess could wait no longer. She stepped back in haughty anger at his rejection.

Next gray-eyed Athene stood before him in her simple dress. Her head was bare of her helmet, and she had laid aside her weapons of war. The little violets about her perfumed

the air as she looked down at him smilingly, yet with a hint of scorn.

"I will teach you all the wisdom that there is in the mind of man" was her promise as her calm eyes looked through him. She understood his simplicity and knew she was not for him.

Paris reddened and dropped his eyes before the gaze of the goddess. He knew nothing of what she had offered, but he felt her contempt and jerked aside a little. The goddess stepped back, not astonished, and yet she was angry too.

Last of all came smiling Aphrodite, around whose white feet grew heavy-scented narcissi and golden daffodils. Her voice was confident and merry as she offered her bribe to him. "You shall have the fairest woman in all the world to wife," said she gently, while her sea-blue eyes laughed into his with a look Paris had often seen on the face of Oenone. Here at last was a goddess whose irresistible charm he understood. Aphrodite put forth her hand for the apple with a gesture as though she would actually touch him. Paris felt her warm fingers meet his for a second as he laid the prize in her palm. Then she was gone, and though he often saw her afterward, she never revealed her full beauty to him again.

Aphrodite was triumphant, but the two other goddesses plotted revenge. First, however, the goddess of beauty did much for her favorite. She told him of his birth, led him into Troy, and caused Priam and Hecuba to forget their fears and to receive him as their son. Paris was accepted as a prince and forgot Oenone, for Aphrodite had murmured in his ear that the beautiful wife was yet to come.

2

Helen

THE house of Menelaus, most powerful of the kings of Greece, lay on the edge of the Spartan plain. Here the evening meal was being prepared for the men of the great household, who were gathering in the courtyard as they returned from vineyard or field. The lowing of cattle filled the air, for milking was over and the great herds of the king were being penned for the night.

A servant came quickly into the dim hall in which the torches were just being kindled. "There is a chariot in the gateway, King Menelaus," he announced. "A young man declares himself to be Paris, Prince of Troy in Asia, traveling to see the world."

"Bring him in," answered the king. "While the women prepare a bath and lay out fresh garments, you may send word to the queen that a stranger will feast with us, for she loves to near talk of far lands."

11

Menelaus rose from his chair by the hearth, but as the guest came into the torchlight, the king hesitated for a moment in amazement at the sight of the young man's exceeding beauty.

Paris seemed all brown and golden. His bright helmet was pushed back, and yellow hair clustered from beneath it round a brown face, ruddy with health. A tawny leopard skin hung over his shoulders. His belt and sandals were of gold. His short tunic was pure white, showing arms and legs lightly tanned. "When he stands beside Helen, my wife," thought Menelaus, "they will make the most beautiful couple that has ever been seen upon earth."

When Paris emerged from his bath, his yellow hair combed and shining, men set a chair for him beside Menelaus and drew up a small table. A girl brought a pitcher of water, which she poured into a silver basin for the washing of hands. Then the carver laid platters of meat before them, while an old servant added wheaten bread, cheese, figs, and other such foods from the storehouse. Another carried in the golden cups and a bowl of wine mixed with water. As the king ate with his guest, he was charmed by the young man's grace and the low tones of his musical voice.

"You must sing for us after the feast," said he. "If your skill with the lyre matches your voice, we shall think ourselves lucky indeed. Our minstrel is old, so that the queen grows weary of his songs and keeps to her room. Without her, gloom descends on my hall."

"I have some skill in music," admitted the young man. "Indeed Hector, my brother, declares that I spend too much

time with my lyre and neglect the weapons of war. I am a
fair shot with a bow, but it is true that I was reared in the
mountains and never trained with spear or sword."

"Each man has a different gift," said the warrior king with
tolerant contempt.

"Indeed that is so," replied Paris earnestly. "Hector's gift
is prowess in war. Mine is mere grace and beauty, yet you
should not despise it, since it alone is not born of practice,
but comes unsought direct from the blessed gods. No man
can win it to whom it has not been given."

"Best of all are the gifts of the gods," said the king mechan-
ically, but his eyes were already on the doorway, where a little
bustle of servants marked the arrival of his wife. A pretty girl
drew up a chair by the hearth, while another knelt to adjust
a soft rug before it. A third wheeled in a silver basket of yarn,
across which lay a distaff full of bright blue wool to be spun.
Behind all these came the lady, Helen. Menelaus looked to
his guest for the gasp of admiration with which strangers were
used to greet the dazzling appearance of the loveliest woman
upon earth. Paris' lips opened and moved slightly, but no
sound came. Menelaus, marveling at the charm of his sudden
smile, missed the little start given by Helen at the sight of so
beautiful a young man. Nor could he hear the voice of
Aphrodite, though it sounded very clearly in Paris' ears: "I
promised you the fairest woman in all the world to wife."

Paris took the lyre to sing a lay for Helen, and her husband
was glad that this evening she lingered in the hall. On the
following nights she stayed late again while Paris wooed her
with whispers and glances, with the notes of his voice as he

sang for her, with a secret touch on her hand. Menelaus, pleased by the gay charm of his guest, thought nothing of his admiration for Helen. All men hung upon the sight of her, yet she, though she loved her husband but little, showed no favor to others. Her nature, the king imagined, was cold.

At last, however, on a moonless night, Helen rose silently from her husband's side to steal down the narrow steps and through the great hall where the sleepers stirred uneasily. In the courtyard, Paris was wheeling out his light chariot, while his servant led the horses through the gateway, where the noise of their harnessing might not be heard. Soon Paris leaped into the chariot and put one arm around Helen as she clung to the rail. The servant sprang aside from the horses' heads. In the dark hall the noise of the wheels was like distant thunder, rolling farther and farther away into the hills.

Down on the coast in the early morning the great ship in which Priam had sent out his favorite son hurriedly hoisted her sails. Her long oars clawed the gray water, even as in his palace in Sparta Menelaus awoke, alone. The most beautiful woman in the world had left her husband. The guest who was treated with honor had robbed his friend.

3

The Madness of Odysseus

THE father of Helen had been a farsighted man. When he saw that his daughter was wooed by every prince in Greece, he determined to make her chosen husband the greatest of them all. He therefore made every suitor take an oath to count Helen's husband as his overlord for the future. It so happened that Menelaus, on whom the king's choice finally fell, was not enterprising and had hitherto made no demand on the services of the kings of Greece. When, however, envoys were sent to fetch back Helen, the Trojans, commercial rivals of Greece, supported Paris. They refused to give up Helen or even to pay a fine. Thereupon Menelaus, goaded on by his more ambitious brother, Agamemnon, sent all the kings a message to meet with him at Aulis, where a fleet was being fitted out to punish Troy.

Great dismay fell on the kings of Greece when this news

was brought to them. It was years since the wooing of Helen. Those who did not win her had put her out of their minds and married others. Now they were husbands and fathers, busy with cares of their kingdoms. Though they were jealous of the power of Troy, they felt that this quarrel was not theirs and that the town was very far away. Kingdoms would have to be left to the management of a struggling wife, of an aged father, or of a half-grown son. The seas were wide and dangerous. Success was uncertain. Although the kings of Greece would not publicly break their oaths, yet it was clear that they did not want to come.

The more the kings wavered, the more determinedly Agamemnon pushed them on. This was his chance to launch the greatest of fleets that the world had seen and to sack the greatest of cities. His messengers were persuasive men, carefully chosen, and Palamedes, the cleverest of them all, was sent to Ithaca, where King Odysseus dwelt.

Odysseus was the wisest man in Greece and the most winning talker. He was broad and burly in appearance, at first sight less impressive than taller men. Words came to him as easily as the snowflakes come in winter, and the notes of his great, deep voice held men spellbound while he played upon their hearts. No man who had heard Odysseus speak could fail to respect him, wherefore Agamemnon had hoped to use him to persuade the other kings.

Unfortunately, of all the kings in Greece, Odysseus was the most unwilling to come. His land was farthest from Troy, since Ithaca was a little island off the western coast, while Troy was across the eastern sea. He loved the rocky country and the simple farmers and fisherman of his home. He longed to stay with his dear wife, Penelope, who had just borne him a son. In the face of these things, his oath seemed quite unreasonable, yet the wise king lacked a good excuse to break it. Therefore about two days before the arrival of Palamedes, Odysseus suddenly went mad.

It was very convincingly done. In spite of their natural suspicions, even the elders were taken in. Early one morning Odysseus was found on the shore driving two oxen harnessed to a plow and turning the dry sand over in furrows. Round his neck was a great bag of salt that he was sowing as he went, muttering wildly to himself. "Must get on with the plowing," he was saying. "Must be done by dark."

People tried to reason with him, but it was no use. His wild eyes looked right through them, and he gave no sign of having heard. A man tried to stop the oxen, but Odysseus drove right on and would have plowed him under if he had not jumped aside. Penelope came down to plead with him, her young son in her arms, but though she implored him to listen and the baby cooed to him, he took no notice. Penelope walked up and down beside him, talking and trying to make him listen all day long. When night came, attendants led her home, but Odysseus merely loosed the oxen and lay down on the furrows. At dawn he was up again, hair and beard matted with sand, plowing along the seashore as before.

This was how Palamedes found him. Distracted men lined the beach and his wife walked beside him carrying the child. The man himself, wild-eyed and dirty, was goading the oxen on and muttering constantly, "Must be done by dark."

Palamedes did not believe in Odysseus' madness. "This is too well timed," he declared with scorn, hoping to arouse the king into betraying anger. Odysseus' face was burned bright red by the sun, so that there was no chance of his changing color, and Palamedes soon found himself as helpless as Penelope had been. He ran up and down by the plowshare in the hot sun, breathlessly repeating the message of Agamemnon. He tried to stop the oxen, but was knocked down and nearly trampled. He appealed to the watching elders, and they simply wrung their hands. He was hot and dirty and bruised where he had fallen beneath the oxen. He was making himself ridiculous, and he knew it. The group of spectators, concerned as they were, began to find him so. Presently some of them laughed.

Palamedes lost his temper. With a bound he jumped on Penelope, snatched her child, and flung it down on the sand straight under the oxen's feet. The crafty king, who had noticed nothing for two days, suddenly and completely gave himself away. He wrenched the plow around with all his strength and then sprang to the heads of the plunging oxen. He snatched his child away from the trampling feet. Then he turned on Palamedes and knocked him down.

It was no use pretending to be mad any more. Odysseus had to come to his senses and listen to the messenger with as much dignity as he could assume. It was he that was ridiculous now.

"I would not be Palamedes," whispered one old man to another as he saw his king's gray eyes rest on Agamemnon's

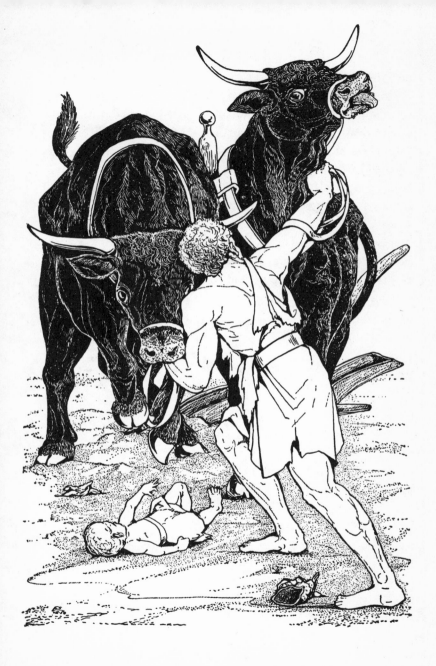

messenger. "No wise man cares to be made to look like a fool, and though Odysseus is a good friend, he is a fearful enemy."

In later years news came to Ithaca that Palamedes had been put to death by the Greeks for having dealings with the Trojans. The old men put their heads together, and their beards wagged busily. "Did we not say our king is a fearful enemy?" they whispered. A rumor then went around that a plot of Odysseus had destroyed an innocent man.

Be that as it may, Odysseus kept his oath to Menelaus and manned his ships. He kissed Penelope good-bye and saw her holding the little boy as she waved to him from the shore. It was twenty years before he had sight of wife or child again.

4

The Discovery of Achilles

WHEN Agamemnon had won over Odysseus, his task with the other kings was far easier. With Odysseus' example and persuasion, they gradually assembled until every king had arrived but one, the greatest hero of all.

This was Achilles, only son of Peleus and Thetis, by this time grown to manhood and now famous for his strength, his speed of foot, and his beauty. Peleus was too old to lead the powerful array of the Myrmidons, but in Achilles could be found a successor. All had heard of Achilles' feats, for he had been brought up by the centaur, Chiron, half horse, half man, who had been tutor to many heroes. Achilles, it was said, could outrace the deer and catch the flying dart that his own hand had flung. He could check a maddened team of horses in full flight, and face a lion or a mad she-bear alone. All knew of his goddess mother and of the tale that her son would be more famous far than his father, the mighty Peleus.

Unfortunately there was another prophecy about Achilles, which silver-footed Thetis had learned from her father, an old, wise sea god. Though her son was to be very famous, his life was to be short. He would die in the height of his glory before the gates of Troy.

Thetis was desperately anxious to cheat the Fates. When her son was a baby, she had taken him down to the gray mud banks of the Styx, which flowed round the land of the dead. She had plunged him into the seething waters that even the ghosts dared not enter, and thereby she had made his flesh immune from death. No weapon could kill him. One heel only was unprotected, where the goddess had gripped her baby as she dipped him in.

Not content with this, Thetis had gone further and tried to make her son immortal. Here she was prevented by Peleus, who did not understand what she was doing and feared for the baby's life. Thetis left her husband in anger at this and went back to the dim depths of the sea. Yet she still watched over Achilles, and to protect him from war she sent him at last to the court of the king of Scyros to be brought up among his daughters. Here Achilles lived in seclusion and because of his youth and beauty passed for a girl when he was dressed like one. In private he might ride and run or throw the javelin, but when he came forward among the princesses and the king said, "These are my daughters," no one could distinguish Achilles, though all knew that one was he.

The messenger of Agamemnon had been sent to summon Achilles, but the king said, "I have only daughters," and closely as the messenger looked, he could not tell to which one he should appeal. They all blushed and looked astonished. Achilles, who was secretly wedded to one of the princesses, Deidamia, had given his word to his wife and mother not to reveal himself. He was therefore silent, although he himself wished to go.

Finally Agamemnon appealed to Odysseus, who thought of a trick to discover the truth. He came as a traveling merchant, not a messenger, asking to display his wares in the palace of the king. At first he showed valuable ornaments: pins, combs, bracelets, women's wear only and too precious for ordinary girls. Presently therefore a servant came to the great hall from the princesses, asking the merchant to bring his goods to the mistresses' room. Attendants picked up the bales and boxes, some of them not yet unpacked, and escorted the merchant across the courtyard to where the princesses sat.

Odysseus watched the girls carefully as they exclaimed over his wares. Each picked up pins and jewels, tried them, paraded with them in gown or hair; yet it seemed to the crafty watcher that one showed less eagerness. Casually he undid another bundle for them. In it lay more trinkets, even rarer than before, but in the midst of them lay a marvelous sword such as a man might dream of all his life and never own.

The third princess could not take her eyes off that sword. She picked up other things and played with them but she always made excuse to put them back. Her fingers went stealthily to the blade, to the hilt when she thought the merchant was not looking. The piles by the sides of the other two grew bigger, but the third princess had chosen nothing yet. At last the merchant feigned departure and began to close his bundles. "I must go now," he said, "but next year I may come again and have more treasures for you. The third princess does not like my wares, however. Is there not anything she would buy?"

The third princess hesitated, then decided to risk it. "Yes," she said clearly, "I will buy the sword."

"You shall have it as a gift," said the merchant, "to a king's son from a king. For you must be Achilles, and I am Odysseus come here with a message for you."

Thus Odysseus delivered his message, and Achilles was glad to be discovered, because he longed for the great adventure. He collected his men and set forth for Aulis, but his goddess mother wept to see him go.

5

Iphigenia

AGAMEMNON lay encamped at Aulis. Black ships were drawn up two deep above the tide mark of seaweed circling the bay. Offshore the boats of late comers swung at anchor, their oars under the benches, and their square sails carefully stowed. By countless smoky campfires, men were boiling pitch, heating metal, cooking whole oxen, or burning sacrifices to the immortal gods. The wind blew steadily in from the sea, carrying the noise of the encampment far over the uplands, whence shepherds could hear the crash of the axes, the clinking of armorers' hammers, the lowing of cattle, and the confused shouts of men. Each day brought fresh arrivals, until there seemed no end to the massed forces of Greece.

Chief among the heroes were Achilles and Odysseus, yet there were many others present of almost equal fame. From the horse-breeding plain of Argos came Diomede, the charioteer. Gigantic Ajax, the prince of Salamis, bore a shield of seven layers of horsehide studded with bronze. It covered its mighty owner from head to foot, and he swung it with ease, though no other man could wield it. With him was his half-brother, Teucer the archer, who was son of a Trojan princess carried away by their father long years before. A second Ajax, son of Oileus, was a famous spearman and after Achilles the swiftest runner in the host. The most respected was white-bearded Nestor of Pylos. He still led his forces in person, although he had warlike sons.

These were the greatest of the chieftains, yet besides them came hundreds more. The mightiest expedition that the world had known lay ready at last, waiting only the changing of the wind.

A favorable wind was long in coming. Day after day it blew steadily in from the east. Food was unpacked and eaten. Men huddled uncomfortably in rude shelters of turf began to murmur. Some of the kings talked openly of going home. Such a storm, they said, was a sign of the gods' ill favor. The truth was they were discontented, for they found Agamemnon highhanded and haughty. "Overlords are better at a distance whence they can make no claims on us," said they.

Agamemnon, who heard the grumbling, realized that his host was likely to melt away. If his army went home without starting, his authority would be over; he would become the laughingstock of all Greece. While the men still held together, it was essential that the wind should change. The king sought out Calchas, the prophet, who knew the mind

of the gods and could foretell the future. "You must tell me
how to win a fair breeze," he said.

Calchas promised to find an answer, but he spent long at
the altars, praying and burning offerings, before he came
gravely back to the king. "We are indeed in the gods' ill
favor. It is better that we go home," he declared.

Agamemnon leaped up in indignation. "That is impossible!" he said, as his staff rang sharply on the ground. "If
none of us is ever to return, we still must sail. Give me a
fair wind and a hope of glory if it cost my kingdom and my
life."

The old man put his hand to his beard in a slow, thought-
ful gesture. "It will indeed cost life," he answered. "The
price is too high, O King. For the last time, disband us and
go home."

"Never!" cried Agamemnon hotly. "Never! do you think
this is a game that I can interrupt as I please? I have staked
everything on this quarrel, and if I fail now, I lose all. What
treasure is too great for the gods to demand of me?"

"Your daughter, Iphigenia," answered the prophet with
his eyes on the ground.

The king laughed with relief and scorn. "I will offer her
gladly," he declared. "I had thought to marry her nobly, but
the gods may make her a priestess if they will."

"She must be slain on the altar of Artemis," said Calchas
distinctly, "as the price of a fair wind."

Agamemnon started in horror. His gay young daughter a
human sacrifice! Her father brought to consent to such a

/deed! No glory the world could offer would wipe away such sin. "It is impossible," he said shortly. "We shall wait here. Sooner or later the wind will change."

The wind did not change, and presently the other chiefs learned the dreadful news from Calchas. Plenty of them were quick to say that they had all offered their lives for a king who would not sacrifice a single one for them in return. Although they did not wish the maiden's death, they were glad to put the blame on Agamemnon for breaking up the host.

At last the king saw that he must take on himself either failure or the greatest of crimes. He was genuinely fond of his daughter, but she was less to him than his pride. He sent a messenger to bring Iphigenia to the camp.

The poor girl came full of eagerness and decked out in her best clothes, for Agamemnon had given as an excuse that he had arranged a match for her with Achilles. In this, however, the king overreached himself somewhat, since his wife, Clytemnestra, insisted on attending the wedding of her child.

Clytemnestra was the sister of Helen and far prouder, though less fair. She now felt just as much rage against Agamemnon as agony at losing her child. The girl herself, stunned at first by the tidings, was at the last pitifully brave. It was the furious mother who hurled at Agamemnon all the reproaches the victim left unsaid. "I will repay you for this hour if it takes me ten years of waiting," she cried.

Agamemnon turned away from her without answering. His mind was made up, and his pride thought little of a woman's threats, though he knew the fierce nature of his queen. He was perhaps more moved by the pleas of Achilles,

who was touched by the young girl's courage and put aside his own hopes of glory to intercede for her. Nevertheless, the king's nature could not bear the reproach of failure, and he hardened his heart.

Iphigenia was led out to the sacrifice. The knife of the slayer rose and fell. Only the gods knew that what seemed her lifeless body was really that of a fawn, since Artemis might demand but would not actually accept such an offering. The goddess snatched up Iphigenia in her arms and carried her off to the far distant land of Tauris to serve as a priestess there.

The corpse lay on the altar. Men looked up from the sacrifice to see the changing of the wind. Instantly all was confusion as each hurried down to his ship, drowning the memory of the deed they had allowed in the thoughts of glory to come. The fleet put out from Aulis, but by their crime the heroes had entered on a war that though glorious, was to be grim. A little urn full of ashes was all that came back to many and many a home. Numbers fell fighting in battle, and the seas drowned countless more.

Ten years passed slowly. In Ithaca, Queen Penelope wept nightly for Odysseus, her lord. In the restless kingdom of the Myrmidons, the failing Peleus struggled vainly for order, longing for the help of his son. In Mycenae, grim Clytemnestra kept her husband's axe sharp and bright. Agamemnon's people looked eagerly for their king's return, and Clytemnestra waited too, that in the moment of her husband's triumph she might murder him.

PART 2

OPENING

1

The Trojan Princes

WATCHMEN stood on the towers of the gateway looking out from the Trojan walls to the distant sea. In the courtyards of the princes throughout the city, men were at work upon armor. Small boys were handing them tools, running for oil for the straps, or crowding about to listen to the history of each piece brought out for repair. The princes alone were not present, but had gathered in the high hall of Priam to determine their answer to the envoys of the approaching Greeks.

Priam sat in the center with the old men near him, and his fifty sons and their cousins were ranged on either side. Old Antenor held the staff of the speaker, but the young men would not listen to him. They thrust out their feet and lay back with open insolence, or turned to speak to one another. Paris made a jest and laughed among his companions. Antenor turned on him, the white staff quivering in his indignant hand. "You told us the Greeks would not come," he remarked with withering contempt.

"I said that Menelaus would not bring them," retorted Paris, scrambling to his feet. "Nor has he. His brother, Agamemnon, leads the host."

"What matter, since they are here?" cried the old man.

"This only," answered Hector, the leader of the brothers, lifting his head from his hand, "that the Greeks have not come here for Helen merely, or Menelaus would have brought them himself. Do you think so mighty an army will go tamely home without fighting after a year of preparation for war?"

"We have just heard Menelaus," said Antenor. "He asked only Helen and satisfaction for wrong."

"Menelaus is a fool," replied Hector briefly. "He can see no further than himself. Princes of Troy, the real envoy of Agamemnon is Odysseus, whom you have just heard. Although he is a marvelous speaker, you must not be deceived by him, for you can see from his own words that the war has already opened. Months ago our father, Priam, sent messengers to the cities of the mainland and to the islands, begging them to uphold our cause. Now the Greek fleet has fallen upon them. Cities have been sacked and queens held to ransom. The king of Thebe and his seven sons have perished for our sake. Men have died in our cause, Trojan leaders, and we cannot now abandon it ourselves."

"Bitter is your sorrow for Thebe," answered Antenor boldly, "but beware lest in your anger you bring the same fate on Troy. Even though Andromache, your wife, has lost father and seven brothers in Thebe, it still does not become you to counsel war in revenge for your private loss."

There were cries of anger from the princes, while Hector, reddened with unspeakable fury, stood struggling for self-control. "Insults come easily in such times," he said at last. "It is but a few moments since Polydamas here declared that I urge war because I hope to win glory as the greatest fighter of you all. Were not this a day of mourning in my household, you both should repent it. As it is, I shall speak no further, but let the voice of the assembled princes decide." He sat down and hid his face once more, while the noise of the princes' indignation gathered on either side.

"I say we shall perish as Thebe has," cried Antenor over the tumult. "The very name of Trojan will disappear from the earth."

"That shall never be," declared grave young Aeneas, son to the goddess Aphrodite by Anchises, who was cousin to the king. "My mother foretells that a great race shall spring from me, and that it shall rule the Greeks themselves and all other peoples, even to the Pillars of Heracles, which lie at the edge of the world."

"Be that as it may," cried the fierce young Troilus, "I and my brothers, who are Priam's sons, rule over you in Troy." He put his hand to his sword and glared at Aeneas, who returned his look with defiance.

Old Priam made a sign to Antenor, and the councilor sat

down frowning, while the king rose slowly to his feet. There was a great dignity about the old man, for he had been a king for fifty years. Even the two angry youths turned from each other, while the murmur and shuffling of the assembly died away.

"Let us not quarrel about the future," said Priam at last in the slow, distinct fashion of an old man who takes pains to be heard. "That still lies in the urns of Zeus, and no man can know what it will be. Our answer to these two envoys concerns us now, and I say it must be war. Hector does not urge battle for his wife's sake, but because we have no other choice. You all know the Greeks sacked Troy before in my boyhood, killed my father, and carried my sister away with them as a slave. I am therefore no lover of Greeks, yet when the first envoys came from Menelaus, I bade you return Helen peaceably. At that time you said Menelaus could not gather an army and that it would shame us to yield to his threats. We defied him, and messengers went out to the cities of our alliance, so that all the East began to prepare for war. Now war is here. Let us destroy the Greeks utterly and leave none of Agamemnon's army to return home and boast of his deeds."

"War is here!" echoed the princes eagerly, but the old men around the king sat silent and grave.

"Hector," said Priam to his son, "shall we fight on the shore or let the Greeks land freely and meet them on the plain outside our gates?"

Hector raised his great head once more and fixed his bright, blue eyes on the king. "On the shore," said he quickly. "Later, if they win a landing, we will destroy them on the open plain. Behind Troy lie the wilds of Mount Ida, so that we are safe from seige, for they will not dare to surround us, lest they be surprised from thence. They must camp on the shore beside their ships, for if we can burn these, they will have no means of escape and will perish utterly."

The princes shouted in applause as they clashed their swords against their armor, for many had come to the council already clothed in the weapons of war. Such a noise arose in the hall that for a time they did not hear the clamor of the trumpets. The watchmen on the gateway towers were shouting. Already the dark sea was dotted with sails, numberless as the petals of a cherry tree scattered by the wind. Folk hurried to the walls and the roofs of the houses, while the clamor of a thousand voices rose on the air.

The temples of the gods stood grouped on the citadel, which was a small, steep eminence rising in the center of the town. There stood the little wooden shrine of Athene, housing an image rudely carved and incredibly old, yet treasured above others. It was said to have fallen from heaven, and a legend declared that as long as it remained on the citadel, Troy would endure. Next to it lay the temple of Apollo, lately built of fair white marble, with a colonnade all around. Even as the princes, roused at last by the clamor, hastened out of the hall of King Priam, Apollo's priestess came out of the shadow of the temple columns and stood regarding them.

The priestess was a tiny figure clothed in pure white, pale as a marble statue. Ash-blonde hair streamed loosely over

her shoulders from beneath the woolen band that marked her sacred office. Cassandra had dedicated herself as priestess and bride of Apollo, who had given her the power of foreseeing the future. Later she had wished to break her vows and marry, in punishment for which Apollo had added the curse that she should never be believed.

The younger princes came running across the square toward the gateway, and Cassandra let them go indifferently, for the message that she had been charged with was not for them. Behind came a group of the older ones moving more slowly, among whom the great head of Hector rose high above the rest. With a sudden gesture, Cassandra tore at her hair, screaming like a madwoman.

"Look!" she cried, pointing at vacancy. "Hector drags dead in the dust behind Greek chariot wheels. See our foes laugh! Troy flames! Woe is me! Agamemnon, fierce Agamemnon!" She shrieked again and again, while Hector beckoned to the temple attendants, who had run out at their mistress' cries.

"Lead her in," he said sternly. "Treat her kindly, but keep her indoors while the madness is on her. It is not fitting that a king's daughter should run screaming about the streets. She is too gentle for war, and terror fills her with wild fancies. Surely her mind will recover when victory comes."

Hector turned to go calmly, though his heart was heavy for the madness of his sister. Moreover, in his melancholy moods he also saw into a future that seemed to him dreadful beyond men's powers of belief. Yet it was too late for peace with honor, so that he smiled as he walked to the ramparts, that all might see their leader was glad to look upon his foes.

2

The Foremost Man

LAODAMIA was so new a bride that the great house her husband had been building for her was still unfinished. The hall was but just roofed over, while the storehouses and sheds for the cattle had not been begun. Nevertheless, her own chamber was completed, though the pieces of the great bed that would stand there lay piled against the wall. Protesilaus himself had been adorning this with pictures beautifully inlaid in gold and ivory, and now his young wife would let no workman lay hand on it. She still slept on the rough pallet hastily put up for her when she and Protesilaus had been wed.

Night was her happiest time, for often she would dream of her husband. Before he sailed for Troy, she had caused a wax mask of his face to be modeled and painted cunningly. Now she made the artist complete the whole figure, which she draped in Protesilaus' garments. Placed in a poor light in the darkest corner of the chamber, it sometimes seemed as though it actually were her husband when she glanced at it quickly. She had a strange superstition that when she could see it in this way at the time of sunset, it would come alive in her dreams that night. Sometimes it actually did this, yet the vision was always oppressive, bringing a dreadful feeling of sadness. Many words would come into her mind, but she could never think which to say. She would gaze on him, and he on her in a despairing, agonized silence, until presently the short night was over, and she was alone.

The old king and queen were gentle with their strange, sad daughter-in-law, but it seemed to them that as yet they hardly knew her. The fact was they were old and had learned that time passes, if slowly. In a year or two when Troy was taken, their son would come back to them again. To Laodamia the years ahead were so black and long that she could not imagine them passing. Try as she would, she was unable to conceive that the time for happiness could return.

For the present she sat long hours in her chamber weeping, or wandered silently through the unfinished courtyards of her home. She put away her rich robes with their bright woven borders and dressed in white like a simple slave or a widow. The old couple shook their heads, dismayed by her thin, bony arms and her peaked face, which looked almost as white as her garments.

At last during the long weeks when the Greek ships lay at Aulis, Laodamia had a different dream. She thought she took the wings of a sea gull and fled out over the ocean to join her lover, she knew not where.

She found him standing in the prow of his ship, clad in full armor. His face looked strange and eager, and he made no sign as she swept down past his head with a scream that was lost in the creak of the oarlocks and a great sound of shouting. Protesilaus shifted his shield as a stone whizzed past.

Now she saw that there were a thousand ships on the sea. The water was black with them. Their long oars crept over the surface like the legs of beetles as they edged in towards the land.

On the beach slingers were working madly, sending volleys of stones about the ships like hail. The shields, however, protected the spearmen, and these stood like bulwarks in front of the rowers, so that the ships came steadily on.

The massed ranks of warriors by the water's edge shifted and parted to a great shout of "Hector!" as a champion strode out before them, armored in glittering bronze. He seemed a huge figure of a man, fully seven feet from the tip of his plume of red horsehair to the straps of his sandals, studded with bronze. His great spear flashed like fire in the sunlight. Over all the noise of the battle, his deep voice could be heard shouting, "Death to the foremost man!"

"Death to the foremost," echoed the masses behind him, and a forest of spears was shaken in the air.

The slingers had ceased their throwing, lest they injure their own men when the battle was joined. Now the creaking of the oars died also, as the ships fell away in confusion, each one unwilling to drive first up the beach. In the sudden lull, the shouts of startled helmsmen rose wildly on the air.

Protesilaus glanced around him. On either side the foremost ships hung back in confusion, while those behind pressed on. Here and there the crash of collision arose. With a sudden gesture he raised his spear in the air and shouted to his rowers. Their oars plunged into the water, and his ship leaped forward onto the land.

"Death to the foremost," yelled the Trojan crowd.

"Immortal fame!" cried Protesilaus, and leaped.

He landed at the edge of the water, stumbling slightly as the loose pebbles shifted underneath his feet. Before he could straighten himself, Hector was upon him. With a great crash the Trojan's spear pierced through both shield and breastplate and bore Protesilaus backward to the ground. His helmet splashed into the shallows and disappeared from sight.

Ships were driving onto the beach now, and all along the edge of the water, battle was joined. Behind the front ranks men were dragging and heaving at Protesilaus. They had him out of the water at last, but Laodamia saw his golden head fall back limply and knew that he was dead.

Strangely enough the terror of this vision did not drive Laodamia to despair. Rather it gave her hope that the gods would have some pity, since they had granted her a vision of the tragedy yet to come. From that time she spent many days at the altars of the gods, particularly of Father Zeus, and Hermes, the messenger of dreams.

"Grant me three hours with my husband after his death," she prayed. "If he must perish, at least bring him back to me for a little while before he goes down to the land of the dead."

Her heavy heart was actually lighter after some time, for she believed that her prayer would be answered. Although she dreamed no more of her husband, she thought this a good sign and left the altars of the gods to wait in her chamber for her lord. She neither ate nor slept any more, it seemed, and was faded to a white, wasted image of herself, but she did not care.

It was the evening of a long summer day that, glancing over her shoulder at the statue, as she so often did, she once more imagined that it moved. Her heart beat high, but she would not look at it again. "It is only an image," she thought. "My husband himself will appear to me in time."

Something stirred in the corner behind her. It was no statue, but Protesilaus himself with dripping hair, leaning heavily on his spear. She leaped to her feet and flung herself into his arms.

A long time was spent in kissing, during which there was no need for words. At last, however, the two sat down, hands linked, while Laodamia leaned against her husband's shoulder. The familiar oppression of her dreams now came over her. In the face of the long parting before them, there was nothing that she could say.

"Have you no word for me?" he asked at last. "I must go down to the daffodil fields of Elysium, where the spirits of dead heroes dwell and where the loves of the shades are as faint as their ghostly figures. While life and strength are still within us, speak to me of our love."

"I cannot speak," said Laodamia in agony. "I do not think my voice will be heard on earth any more. Wait for me in the daffodil valleys, for you may be sure I shall follow you soon." /

He loosened her hands and got up slowly. A long, last look passed between them. "Come soon," he said quietly at last. "The memories of the shades grow faint in the dim land of Hades. Happier are the meanest slaves on earth than the ghosts in the valleys of Elysium. Come soon, lest I forget."

She opened her pale lips to answer, but her husband was gone and only the waxen image stood stiffly where he had been. Laodamia sank down on her bed, not weeping, but broken in spirit. Turning her face to the wall, she lay there without movement or speech until she died.

The Greeks in Troyland, when their footing was won and the black ships lay on the beach, made a grave mound for Protesilaus. Within it they buried his ashes and also his armor, for they said, "It was a brave leap. He was truly the foremost to win immortal fame. It is fitting to send such a hero down in state to the land of the dead."

3

The Host Musters

THE black ships lay side by side on the beach. Through the huts and tents of the army rang the voices of criers, calling the heroes to battle at Agamemnon's command. Agamemnon himself, clad in his armor but holding his silver sceptre of lordship instead of his spear, walked down the rows of the huts, inspecting his muster. Where he saw men forward in preparation, he praised them, but if any were still unready for war, he was quick to rebuke.

First he came to the tents of Diomede, where the servants were binding the car of a bright painted chariot onto its framework. Beside them, the charioteer was holding two glorious white horses, the leather of whose harness was studded with silver and gold. Diomede himself by the door of his hut was putting on his helmet, while out of the tents of his followers, men rushed like a swarm of bees.

Next to Diomede stood the great Ajax. His men fought on foot, since they came from a small, rocky island unsuited for the breeding of horses. So huge was this hero that the tallest of his men hardly reached the chin strap of his helmet. His great shield of leather and bronze hung by a broad band from his shoulder, covering him almost to the ground. Beside him, scarcely higher than his elbow, stood Teucer, his brother, armed with a bow of polished horn and a quiver of arrows. Teucer bore no armor at all, not even a breastplate, for he hid behind the shield of his brother. Together the two were a deadly pair.

Agamemnon passed beyond Ajax and Teucer, by noble Odysseus, who was fastening the silver clasps of his greaves around his ankles. Beyond him stood Ajax the less, son of Oileus. His warriors were ready, for they were unarmored slingers and archers. A wolfskin hung round each man's neck by the forepaws and made a rough shield for him. With his left hand he could stretch the lower edge tight and hold it away from his body to protect him from missiles. Each carried a sling of twisted strips of cloth and a pouch full of stones, or a bow and a quiver of arrows. Agamemnon passed them in silence, caring little for such light-armed fighters who never dared come to close quarters with the ranks of the spearmen. Behind him they murmured because he had not praised their array.

Next to these lay the tents of Achilles. Here the servants were rubbing his horses, but he himself sat by the door of his tent while captive girls brought him wine. Around him the stewards served meat to his people, regardless of the voices of the criers and the bustle of the great host mustering for war.

"Son of Peleus," cried Agamemnon halting, "for a long time you have been boasting that you and your people are foremost in war. Now Ajax and Diomede stand ready, while you sit at your ease. Perhaps you fear to face Hector, lest he prove the better man and rob you of glory. Talk no more to me of your goddess mother. It is deeds, not words, that are needed to prove you goddess-born."

The fair young face of Achilles grew grim as the winter. "Speak not to me, shameless king, of my courage," cried he. "I have proved it on Thebe. Where were you when that city was taken and the king's seven sons fell to the might of my arm?"

"In my place," retorted the king. "At the head of my host."

Achilles laughed. "It is a great thing, no doubt, to be king," answered he. "A king stays at the head of his army while he sends other heroes out on expeditions. Yet when they capture cities, he takes the best of the booty, for he is the king."

"Does he?" replied Agamemnon, scarlet with anger. "I would not have thought it. Yonder captive youth with the purple and gold on his tunic was never brought forward with the plunder from Thebe which you spread out for the choice of the king."

Achilles rose menacingly. "I kept back no plunder. This youth is not prisoner from there."

"Where then did you take him?"

Achilles smiled. "The king slept soundly last night," he answered mockingly. "Perhaps in the darkness Hermes, messenger of Zeus, will bring him a dream. The dreams of kings are important and must not be missed. A mere hero who is son to a goddess has less need of sleep. Know that this youth is Trojan, not Theban. His name is Lykaon, and I caught him this night in an orchard behind Troy on the foothills of Ida, where he was cutting the wild fig shoots which they use for chariot rails."

"You have been behind Troy?" cried the king in amazement.

"Behind Troy?" said he. "I have been round it. Never again will the Trojans feel safe upon Ida. Aeneas, Anchises' son, was out herding their cattle. He left them and fled over the hills, though he never could have escaped me, had it not been for the dark. As it is, I have brought back some booty and this boy, who is Priam's son."

"You should have killed him," declared Agamemnon. "We cannot keep prisoners, especially the sons of the king."

"He is a child," said Achilles easily. "Can I murder such? I will sell him overseas for a slave if you fear him. But now, O King, I and my men are weary and have not yet eaten. When we go out to battle, you shall witness our valor, but meanwhile pass on and give orders to men who do not know how to fight for themselves."

As Agamemnon choked back his fury, he saw Palamedes, who was encamped next Achilles, laugh with his fellows as he listened to the quarrel. The king went on in silence, for he knew already that Palamedes desired to be commander in chief.

Out of the tents and huts poured men, innumerable as the leaves of an oak tree or as the flowers on the plain of Skamander, where they fought. Athene, daughter of Zeus, had put off her many-colored garments of peace which her own hands had woven, and now stalked through the camp in full armor, inflaming men's hearts, though unseen. Earth groaned like thunder with the drumming of hooves and the thudding of feet as the heroes in their flashing armor of bronze advanced like a forest fire.

On a little mound across the plain, where the view was better than from the walls, stood the swift-footed sentinels of Troy. Now these sped to the city with warning, and the gates opened wide. Out poured the Trojan host, shouting strange cries like a great flock of birds. From the cities of Asia there were kings without number. From the distant steppes came wandering tribes who dressed in skins and lived on mares' milk. Dark warriors followed their chieftains from far Ethiopia, which was said to lie at the edge of the world.

High overhead the invisible gods ranged themselves on this side or that. Above the Greeks hovered Poseidon, the sea king, and with him were Hera, Athene, Hephaistos, and Hermes, the messenger of Zeus. Over the Trojans towered golden Apollo, beside whom stood Ares, Artemis, and Skamander, the god of the yellow river rolling through the Trojan plain.

Now Zeus, the father of gods and men, thundered terribly, and the mountain of Ida trembled along all her wooded crests. With a great clash battle was joined. In wild confusion the cries of the victors, the screams of frightened horses, and the groans of the dying mingled on the air. The red plumes of the fighters met and tossed like two racing torrents in flood.

On the right hand of the raging battle, Diomede scattered the Trojans, but Hector fell on the Greek center like a lion on a huddle of sheep, driving Agamemnon and Ajax before him until Diomede ceased from pursuit and returned to their aid. On the left hand, the Trojan allies, headed by huge Cycnus, pushed back the light forces in front of them almost as far as the ships. At this Achilles, seeing the disaster, called to his Myrmidons and hurled himself into the fray. He came charging out into the battle in a chariot drawn by white horses, looking like the dazzling Apollo himself. The Trojan allies fell back in dismay behind Cycnus, who, vast and unterrified, met the chariot in mid-career.

The fearful spear of Achilles, too huge for other men, flashed through the air and burst through Cycnus' shield and breastplate, but he plucked it out with a laugh. Cycnus' own weapon struck the shield of Achilles with such fearful force that its owner staggered, and the charioteer reined his horses to a stop in a cloud of dust, lest his master be hurled to the ground.

"Your armor may be the better," mocked Cycnus, "but you need it more. I wear mine merely for show, since I am a son of Poseidon, and no weapon can pierce me." He lowered his shield to expose his arm and shoulder.

"Take back your spear," said Achilles between his teeth, and he flung it with all his strength. The weapon merely rebounded from Cycnus' uncovered arm without leaving a mark. Cycnus threw back his head and laughed.

Achilles, drawing his sword, hurled himself right over the rail of his chariot onto his foe. "I can at least hew your armor to pieces about your ears," cried he. Suiting the action to the word, he began to batter at the helmet and shield of his enemy with such force and speed that Cycnus gave ground, half stunned, while great fragments of leather or bronze flew into the air.

Cycnus dropped the useless remains of his shield and raised his sword to ward off the hail of blows. These now fell on his face and helmet so thickly that he retreated faster and faster, dizzy and blinded, seeking in vain some means of escape. Suddenly he tripped over a loose stone and fell backward. Achilles was on top of him in a moment, his great shield crushing the giant's powerful chest. Dropping his sword, the hero leaned forward and twisted his hands in the straps of his enemy's helmet. "If you cannot bleed, you shall choke to death," gasped he.

In another moment all was over. The Trojan allies, seeing their leader dead, fled yelling before the savage Myrmidons. Achilles, stooping over his foe to strip off the remains of his armor, fumbled helplessly for a moment and found himself looking at the bare grass where the body had lain. Though Poseidon could not save his son from a fated death, he would not permit Achilles to triumph over his body. Snatching Cycnus away in his arms, he set him down in his home, where his friends might give him burial.

Achilles looked around and beheld that Hector was once again driving back the Greeks in the center. He stopped the pursuit of the Myrmidons, but before he could bring help, Hector also had recoiled to aid his battered wings. As night was falling, both sides drew back appalled by the slaughter. The Greeks retreated to their camp, and the Trojans to the city. All night long funeral fires burned by the seashore, while the mourning cries of women rose on the air in Troy.

4

Troilus and Cressida

THE story of Troilus and Cressida describes the Greek prophet Calchas as a Trojan deserter. Being sent on an embassy to the Greeks at Aulis, Calchas learned from the gods in a vision that they considered the Greek cause just, and that it would prevail. He therefore threw in his lot with Agamemnon, leaving his countrymen to their fate.

The news of this desertion was received in Troy with great anger. Calchas had left his daughter, Cressida, in the care of her uncle, Pandarus. Prudently she now kept to her house, seeing few people, and was wise enough to appear glad when the Trojans refused to give her up to her father. By such careful behavior she won friends to protect her and lived quietly in Troy in spite of the war until Troilus, bravest of the younger princes, fell madly in love with her.

It was far from Cressida's intention to attract envy to herself by gaining the love of the strongest and handsomest of

Priam's unmarried sons. She was flattered, it is true, but her head was not easily turned. Since she never appeared in company, Troilus could not seek her out. Now she would not even walk abroad in the city until the men had gone out to battle.

Almost daily the old men and the women gathered on the city walls to watch the distant struggle between the Greeks and the Trojans on the plain. Cressida hated the publicity of such places, for the former friends of her father looked on her pityingly, and his enemies whispered to one another at her approach. Nevertheless something drove her, for she had a boundless love for gallantry and daring. Her face would flame with pride when Troilus drove back to the city in triumph, holding up some bright shield or rich breastplate he had stripped from an enemy. Yet when others streamed down to the gates to greet the victorious hero, Cressida veiled her face and went home, lest he should catch sight of her.

This care on the part of Cressida did not dampen Troilus' love, but rather inflamed it. Having no chance to speak to his lady, he appealed instead to her uncle, who in her father's absence was her guardian.

Pandarus, an ambitious man, was happy to advance his fortunes by a match between his niece and one of Priam's most popular sons. There was a chance that the kingdom might come to Troilus. Already one of the princes had been captured and two slain. Anything might happen in war. Pandarus secretly encouraged Calchas' enemies to speak openly against Cressida, for he wished an excuse to form a league of Cressida's friends.

All went according to plan. The frightened Cressida was

easily brought to a gathering of her friends at the house of Prince Deiphobus. Here the cunning of Pandarus won Troilus some minutes alone with his lady. Cressida, confused and grateful, did not strongly reject him. Another interview brought better understanding, and Cressida admitted her love.

There followed a happy time of stolen meetings. Now Cressida sang soft songs as she sat at her loom or combed the bright hair that was her greatest beauty. Every day she smiled down from the walls at Troilus, who would push back his battered helmet from his forehead, glowing with pride. He became a champion of champions. He won a great black shield studded with silver stars, which disappeared after he had carried it in triumph through the city. Some women whispered that it was to be found in Cressida's hall.

"Openhanded as Troilus" became a saying in Troy at this time. Troilus, who had always been respected in war, was now suddenly popular. Women remarked on his swaggering plumes and his gorgeous armor. Men talked of him as second to Hector. Other princes with ambitions, such as the dark young Aeneas, frowned.

In the meantime Calchas had by no means ceased his efforts to regain his daughter. When an important Trojan noble was finally taken prisoner, he appealed to Agamemnon, who agreed to offer the captive in exchange for Cressida.

"I will go on this errand to the Trojans," volunteered the handsome Diomede. "I hear that Cressida is beautiful and has hair as golden as Helen's. I may earn a smile for her rescue, unless she has a lover in Troy."

"Cressida is prudent," replied Calchas easily, "and has

lived in retirement, favoring no Trojan. Like a true daughter, she reserves her smiles for her father's friends."

King Priam readily agreed to the terms brought by Diomede, since he was eager to rescue a valiant noble and cared nothing for Cressida. Hector also consented, though sadly, for he knew of Troilus' secret. "This is hard for the maiden, who wished to remain with us," he said. "I must at least go ahead to break the news."

Troilus was actually with Cressida, as his brother had suspected, and nothing would console his mad grief. He clung to his lady, swearing that he would not let her go. Cressida for her part was quiet, though very pale. "Trust me," she said to comfort him. "Have I not sworn that the sun shall fall from the heavens and the rocks split on Ida before I betray you?"

"How shall I live if you leave me?" cried Troilus in agony.

"Trust me," she said again. "I know how to deceive my father. I have thought of a story that will persuade him to send me back as soon as he may."

"How soon?" cried he eagerly, alight with sudden hope.

"In ten days," she answered with confidence. "On the tenth day I swear to return."

Troilus pressed her in his arms again, but Hector, hearing the arrival of Diomede, tore the two lovers apart.

Cressida gave a little start of surprise on meeting Diomede. He and Troilus were at first sight much alike. Both were yellow-haired, blue-eyed, and unusually tall, though Diomede was broader and ruddier. He smiled at Cressida with an air of good-humored self-confidence, and Troilus hated him for it.

"The lady, Cressida, is beloved in Troy," said Troilus stiffly. "If any harm happens to her at your hands, beware. I will kill you and throw you to the vultures, even though the whole Greek army stand in my way."

"I make no promises," said Diomede carelessly, amused at the threat.

"Promise!" shouted Troilus violently, putting a hand to his sword.

"Be quiet, Troilus," said Hector gently. "What harm should he do her? Remember, he is taking her to her father."

Diomede smiled slyly at Cressida, who blushed in annoyance at her lover's ridiculous talk. "I shall go very willingly with Diomede," she said clearly, giving her hand to the Greek. "I am honored that my father sends so valiant a hero."

"Cressida!" cried Troilus despairingly. She halted, half turned away.

"In ten days?" he questioned.

Cressida turned indignantly from him. "You have my word," she said.

Troilus and Pandarus were up with the dawn on the tenth morning and took their stations on the walls above the gate. The Greeks lay encamped far off by their ships, so that there was traffic through the gate all day long unless the swift watchmen from the plain reported that the enemy was advancing to battle. Sheep and oxen grazed outside the walls with herdsmen in attendance. Women went out to wash clothes in the Skamander. Messengers set forth to the cities who had sent contingents to Priam. The soldiers in charge of the gate lounged at their ease, since for a long time no one approached.

"I see a cloud of dust on the hillside," cried Troilus at last, straining his eyes at the distance.

"Why on the hillside?" grumbled Pandarus. "Cressida comes from the shore."

"True." His companion fell silent. Pandarus stole a look at him. His lean, long face had sharpened, and there were red rims to his eyes. He moved incessantly, now leaning over the wall, now shading his eyes, now pacing impatiently. Pandarus sighed.

"He will kill himself if she does not come," he thought. His heart was heavy, for he loved Troilus, and besides, his own fortunes were at stake.

"Someone from the plain!" cried Pandarus sharply. Troilus ran to the wall.

"They have relieved the watchman on the mound," he said in disgust. "It is only the man coming home."

The sun passed the zenith and sank. The chattering women from Skamander had returned.

"She will not come," said Pandarus finally. "Perhaps she could not."

"She must come," insisted Troilus. "We will wait till dark."

Herdsmen drove in the cattle. In the west, the sky was red. Below them the guards were lighting torches and lazily dropping the big bars of the gates into place. Someone had kindled a fire, and a smell of cooking meat arose.

"It is quite dark now, and the gates are shut," said Pandarus. "She cannot come."

"She will steal out in the night and batter on the gate for

admission. Go home, Pandarus, but let me watch, lest the guards do not open to her."

"I will stay," groaned Pandarus, shivering in the cool night air.

Twice in that long night a sheep that had escaped the herdsmen came wandering across the ground below the wall. The second time it did so, Troilus aroused the watchmen and bade them unbar.

"Not for Hector himself," said the leader stoutly. "It is his own order."

The sheep bleated outside with a lost, lonely sound. Troilus drew his sword and set the point to the man's throat. "Unbar," he cried.

A soldier struck up his weapon. Pandarus seized him by the arm. "Come home, Troilus," he said. "Do not you hear it is a sheep? She cannot come."

"She does not wish to come," said Troilus slowly. "When I saw her go out with Diomede, I knew it would be so." He turned away from the wall.

The next morning Troilus was ill. Even after some days when the fighting was renewed, he lay on his bed and would not stir.

"Diomede was in the battle," said Pandarus to him that evening.

Troilus roused himself at once. "She smiled on that great, red lout," he said fiercely, remembering. "A woman who will deceive her father may betray her lover too."

"Did the sun yet fall from the heavens or rocks roll down from Ida?"

"She lied when she swore that oath. Let me die." Troilus turned his face to the wall until Pandarus left him.

Nevertheless, his friend had aroused him. Anger burned in him all that night, and when day broke, he got to his feet. He was so weak with starvation, however, that he could not bear the weight of his armor. When he saw this, he sank back on his bed and called for wine. The servants brought food, and he ate it, and then immediately fell asleep.

He awoke to a great sound of cheering. "It is Deiphobus," said the servant whom he had impatiently summoned. "Deiphobus has wounded Diomede and taken his shield. He is bringing it into the city."

Troilus felt great disappointment. "Deiphobus took the red shield of Diomede?" he inquired.

The servant hesitated. "The shield is black," he said at last, "but it is Diomede's."

"Diomede carries a red shield with a golden boar," said Troilus sharply.

"Diomede carried a black shield studded with silver stars today," said Pandarus from the doorway. "It is the one Cressida took to the Greek camp with her gear."

There was a long silence.

"The sun has dropped from my heaven, Pandarus," said Troilus heavily. "She gave it to Diomede, is it not so?"

"She has forsaken you," agreed his friend gloomily. "Diomede will recover, and you may yet take your revenge."

"What use to fight with Diomede if Cressida nurses him? I shall seek out Achilles in battle. His hands give certain death, and it will be better so."

5

The Time of Discouragement

RAIN fell. Campfires were extinguished, and men huddled in the huts and tents. Outside in their rough shelters the horses moved uneasily in the mud. A few scattered sentries with skins thrown over their backs for protection peered miserably into the dark. Behind them faint glimmers of light showed where in some of the huts men were wakeful, but all sound of gossip or laughter was drowned in the drumming of rain.

The campaign of the Greeks against Troy had gone neither well nor badly. In the field they were superior to the Trojans, though these drew so many allies from the cities around that their numbers had not yet been lessened. Achilles had headed expeditions against the neighboring cities and islands, partly to drain the Trojans of strength, and partly to exact tribute of food and supplies for the Greek host encamped on the shore. Some cities had paid; others had resisted. Twenty-three of these latter had been taken, and the camp was filled with all kinds of booty. Every chief was rich.

For all these reasons the wiser heroes felt certain of capturing Troy, yet even they had begun to question whether victory would be worth the cost. Years had dragged on — summers and winters of huddling in rude shelters on the beach. Heroes fell daily in battle. Now and then there was sickness in the camp. Meanwhile, the fall of Troy lay months or years ahead.

In the midst of such difficulties resentment grew daily against Agamemnon, who had planned the expedition and who was blamed for all its misfortunes. Factions arose in the camp, some men desiring to go home, while others wished to put forward a new commander-in-chief.

The head of this latter party, Palamedes, was Agamemnon's earliest supporter and one of the cleverest men in the host. It was he who had unmasked the pretended madness of Odysseus and persuaded many other kings to obey Agamemnon's call. When the fleet assembled, however, Palamedes found himself less influential than Ajax, or Diomede, or his personal enemy, Odysseus. Infuriated by this treatment, he plotted to put aside Agamemnon and become commander himself.

During the long, wet winter, discontent had mounted to its height. Seizing a moment when Achilles and several other chiefs were absent on forays, Palamedes called an assembly that voted him commander-in-chief amid a storm of applause.

Agamemnon, surrounded by his enemies, went to his hut without a word of protest. However, now that he was back among his own people, it was clear that the commands of Palamedes would have no weight with him.

A gleam of light from Agamemnon's hut widened for a moment as someone slipped in through the curtain of skins that hung before his door. Agamemnon looked up, but said nothing. Odysseus put aside his wet cloak and drew up a chair beside the king's. The single torch cast a shadow on the wall of the two heads bent close together, while the splashing water from the eaves outside deafened any listening ears.

Odysseus curved his hand around his mouth. "I have set going a rumor that Palamedes has sold us to the Trojans," said he softly into Agamemnon's ear. "Even on a night like this such stories fly wildly around the camp. Tomorrow you may call an assembly and accuse him, demanding his death."

"They will not believe me."

"They will at least examine his tent. There is Trojan gold hidden beneath it."

Agamemnon started and sat up. "How do you know?" he demanded sharply.

"I buried it there. It will kill him, never fear."

Agamemnon laughed scornfully. "You have always hated Palamedes," he sneered, "but that is no reason to make me accomplish his murder for you. Palamedes is innocent of treachery. As for his command of the army, it cannot last in any case, since the heroes will never obey him. Why should I stoop to destroy him by such means?"

"One innocent man must die for the people's sake," replied Odysseus earnestly. "We stand on the edge of destruction as it is. Already Ajax swears he will not fight for Palamedes, who is no better than he, but will take his men and go home."

"And Palamedes?"

"Palamedes is mad with ambition. There will be fighting between the chieftains before any ships can put out to sea. Meanwhile, the Trojans will not stand by idle if we come to blows with one another. We shall be lucky if a single ship escapes to Greece."

Agamemnon shifted uneasily. "I admit the danger, but I do not like such plots. Palamedes is not guilty, and moreover he is your private enemy."

Odysseus shrugged. "You imagine I take this sort of revenge on my opponents?" he said. "Well, it does not matter what you think, and it is true that one way or another my enemies come to a bad end. I had not supposed, however, that you were the man to throw the death of the innocent in my teeth. Palamedes has at least conspired against his commander, whereas Iphigenia — "

The king raised his head sharply, interrupting. "I will call the assembly tomorrow," he declared, "and do you play your part. We must act quickly before there is fighting. If it is for the people's sake, let him die."

PART 3

THE WRATH
OF ACHILLES

1

The Quarrel

DOWN from the peaks of Olympus swept Apollo in wrath, while the dreadful arrows of pestilence clanged in his quiver. Descending on the foot-hills of Ida, he sighted the Greek camp, and his silver bow hummed deeply as the arrows flew to their mark. First the mules died, and the dogs. Later the god aimed at men, and for nine days funeral fires burned unceasingly. There was murmuring against Agamemnon because he made no move to appease the god's anger, but the truth was, the king suspected that he himself had been its cause.

On the tenth day Achilles summoned the folk to assembly because Agamemnon would not. This was the first time since the death of Palamedes that a lesser chief had dared send criers through the camp, so that fear and fury were in Agamemnon's heart.

The place of assembly was buzzing like a hive of bees. For a long time the voices of the criers could not silence the tumult, nor induce the excited people to sit still on the benches. When at last Achilles stood up, holding the staff of the speaker, there was a sudden hush, for all were amazed at his boldness and eager to hear what he would say.

Achilles immediately called up Calchas, the prophet, to tell the people the cause of the pestilence, but the old man was afraid to speak out. "Promise me protection if I tell you the truth," he demanded. "I fear lest I draw down the anger of one whom many kings obey."

"No man shall offer you violence and live," Achilles reassured him. "Not even Agamemnon, if it is his anger you fear."

A murmur ran through the ranks of the people at this open challenge, but the prophet, seeing that Agamemnon sat silent, was emboldened to speak out.

"Apollo is angry on account of his servant, old Chryses, the priest, who came lately with great gifts to ransom his daughter from King Agamemnon, whose captive she is. The king refused to let the girl go and insulted her father, in punishment for which Apollo smites us with pestilence. Only when we return the maiden, Chryseis, to her father, will the sickness be cured."

Countless accusing eyes were turned angrily on King Agamemnon, who, seeing that he had been put in the wrong, began to bluster as best he could. "False prophet and maker of trouble," he shouted at Calchas, "who bribed you to lay the sorrows of the Greeks at my door? I will give up Chryseis willingly for the good of the people, though she is the prize of honor which the chieftains awarded me. However, I am your overlord and must have some prize for my dignity's sake. Let the chiefs make me ready another out of the spoils in the camp."

"There is nothing to give you, greedy king," retorted Achilles, springing to his feet. "All the plunder in the camp is divided already. Wait until another city is taken, and you shall have some fair reward."

"You forget your overlord," cried Agamemnon, scarlet. "Who gave you leave to call this assembly, protect your own favorites, and demand my booty from me? If the chiefs refuse me a prize, I am their master and will take one, perhaps from Ajax, or Odysseus, or even from you."

"You dare not take from me fair Briseis, my prize of honor," cried Achilles, beside himself with fury at the suggestion.

"I dare," shouted Agamemnon. "And I will."

The hum that ran through the assembly died to silence as Achilles laid his hand to his sword and looked around for supporters. No other chieftain wished to quarrel with the most powerful of kings. The veins on Achilles' forehead swelled with rage, and his face grew red as fire. He had actually started to spring on his enemy when the goddess Athene, who stood suddenly behind him, caught him back by his golden hair. Men watched him struggle with his fury, but the goddess they did not see.

"For years I have fought here in your quarrel," said Achilles at last, as he let fall his sword. "What harm did Troy ever do me? Fight without my aid for the future, while I laugh to watch you lose. You will suffer fearful defeat for the loss of my valor, just as surely as this staff in my hand will never grow into a tree. Bitter repentance will not stave off the disaster that you have brought on yourself and the host." He dashed the staff furiously to earth and sat down.

Old Nestor arose to appeal to both chieftains for patience, but neither would listen. Agamemnon vowed he would seize fair Briseis. Achilles insisted he would fight no more for the king. As the assembly broke up in confusion, Agamemnon called for his guards.

Achilles went down to the seashore and sat looking out over the gray waters, calling to his mother, the goddess, who rose like a mist from the dim depths of the sea. "My son," said she, stroking him gently, "tell me of your sorrow."

"Mother," cried he, "if my life is to be a short one, should I not have all that I want? You have promised me measureless glory, in spite of which I am now put helplessly to shame. Since in a year or two I must die, the gods owe me my happiness now."

"Bitter is your sorrow to me," answered Thetis. "Unlucky was the hour of your birth. Truly since your life is so short, the gods should grant you what you desire. Let me go to Olympus and pray Zeus to give victory to the Trojans as long as you stay out of the battle. He loves me and will grant what I ask, never fear. You shall make your own terms with Agamemnon."

"Terms?" cried Achilles in fury. "I will laugh when he begs for them."

"Listen for the thunder," said Thetis, "when Zeus nods his head to my prayer."

The gray goddess vanished into air, but Achilles sat still by the shore. Tears came into his eyes for the loss of Briseis, since after his fashion he loved her. Yet the loss of her mainly hurt his pride. She was the first thing he desired that was ever denied him.

2

The Combat

DOWN by the seashore the people of Achilles were competing with javelin or discus. His horses stood quietly at their mangers, and his chariot lay in its shelter well covered up. From the tents and huts of the other kings, however, the forces of the Greeks were going out to battle. Once more the gates of Troy swung wide. The plain was filled with men and horses and was ablaze with bronze. Earth thundered beneath the feet of the armies as they rushed into the fray.

Paris, beautiful as Apollo, sprang out in front of the Trojans. A black panther skin was flung over his shoulders, and his curved bow was slung at his back. In each hand he brandished a bronze-headed spear, and he called on the chieftains of Greece to meet him in combat. Paris was not often seen in the front of the battle, for which reason many of the princes were complaining that they fought in the cause of a coward. Spurred on by their insults, Paris now ran out in front of the army, intending to hurl both his spears and retreat safely into the ranks.

With a great shout, warlike Menelaus leaped from his chariot as a lion leaps on a deer, but Paris knew him and started back in dismay as though he had trodden on a snake. His ruddy cheeks lost their color, and he shrank back behind the shields of the spearmen. Menelaus cried furiously after him, while the other Greek chieftains laughed.

"This war is fought on your account," cried Hector, turning to his brother, "and yet you are not ashamed to make us a mockery to the Greeks by your cowardice. I warn you that the Trojans will not endure you for ever. Your beauty and your singing will not save you on the day when you lie in the dust."

"Bear with me, brother," said Paris earnestly, for much as he feared Menelaus, he dreaded the ill will of the Trojans yet more. "Do not blame me because the gods gave me beauty, while they bestowed prowess in war upon you. Bid the Trojans sit down, and likewise the Greeks, while Menelaus and I fight out our quarrel. The winner shall take Helen, while the losing side shall pay a great ransom. This will settle the struggle with honor, and the Greeks may go home."

Hector made him no answer, but leaped out ahead of the Trojans, taking his spear by the middle in an attempt to halt their onrush. The front ranks stopped in confusion, whereupon the missiles of the Greeks slackened also. In a short time both armies were silent to hear what Hector would say.

Menelaus gladly accepted the offer of Paris, and the chiefs

of each side bade their men sit down on the ground. A messenger hurried to the city to bring out old Priam, so that he
and Agamemnon might make solemn oaths on their people's
behalf.

Priam was sitting on the walls of the city amid the old men
and the women. Even Helen had heard some strange thing
was afoot and had come to look out over the plain. As she
passed by the rows of the elders, they remembered the sons
who had bled and died in her cause. They watched her,
hating her in silence, until as she walked the wind fluttered
back the veil from her face. They sighed as their dim eyes
looked once more on the loveliest of women, and when she
had gone by, they spoke softly among themselves. "Small
wonder," they said, "that both Trojans and Greeks have
suffered so long for her sake."

While the champions were putting on their armor, the
kings of either side prepared sacrifices. On behalf of his people each swore to abide by the truce, calling upon Zeus to
bring vengeance if it were broken. Two men measured out a
grassy space, in which Paris and Menelaus stood up to face
each other.

Paris, who was chosen by lot to throw first, lifted up his
spear and hurled it with all his strength. The weapon struck
Menelaus' shield on the center boss, where it was strongest,
and rebounded onto the grass. Menelaus in turn raised his
arm. With a fearful crash his spear burst clear through Paris'
shield and thudded against his breastplate. Paris twisted to
escape the full force of the blow, yet even so he went stagger-
ing backward.

Menelaus bounded forward, snatching out his sword, and struck before his enemy could recover his balance. Paris ducked his head and received the blow on the crest of his helmet, on which Menelaus' sword broke in three pieces, leaving nothing but the hilt in its owner's grasp.

Once again Menelaus leaped wildly, this time with bare hands. He seized his half stunned foe by the horsehair crest and pulled savagely. Paris fell forward, half strangled by the embroidered strap under his chin. With a shout Menelaus began to drag him over the ground toward the Greeks.

Paris clutched at the strap, gasping heavily. His face turned red, then purple, while his legs twisted in agony. Suddenly the strap burst. Menelaus staggered heavily backward, clutching the helmet. A cloud descended upon Paris, and when it lifted, he was gone. The goddess Aphrodite had snatched up her favorite and borne him unseen into Troy.

Menelaus tossed the helmet to his comrades and turned madly on the Trojans, suspecting they had concealed their champion to save themselves from defeat. "No matter where you hide him, the victory is ours," cried Agamemnon. "Give us back Helen and pay ransom for your city, as you have agreed."

The Trojans stood up in confusion as Menelaus came forward. Each thought that some other man had concealed Paris, but since he was still living, all were unwilling to admit their defeat and pay measureless ransom. There were many wild shouts of refusal, while Menelaus strode up and down, raging like a dog who is seeking the trail.

"There stands Menelaus," thought Pandarus. "The war

would be over if I dared strike one blow for our city." With that he dodged behind the rows of the spearmen and aimed his bow. Menelaus' last hour would now have come, had not the treacherous arrow struck the buckle of the belt which he wore above his corselet. Though two layers thus protected him, the arrow pierced them both and wounded him slightly. Both armies saw the blood flow.

The Greeks raised a terrible shout and leaped into battle, calling upon Zeus to punish their enemies for breaking their oath. They fell upon the mass of the Trojans like an irresistible wave of the sea.

3

Hector and Andromache

THE Greeks surged forward, shouting. Had it not
been for Hector, the Trojans would have been
chased in confusion to the very gates of Troy.
Hector stood like a rock, and soon his men rallied
around him, though their raging enemies pressed them hard.
For a while the battle swayed back and forth, until the furious strength of Diomede put the Trojans before him to flight.
At that, Helenus, a prince of the Trojans who was their chief
prophet, came over to Hector.

"Brother," he cried, "we need more than valor to overcome
a Greek who is favored by the gods. Go back to Troy and bid
your mother lead the women into the temples with offerings.
Their prayers will avail us more at this moment than your
strength, great though it is. I foresee Zeus is ready to grant us
the power to drive the Greeks back over the plain and set fire
to their ships."

"I will go," answered Hector, "but do you and Deiphobus rally the Trojans until my return."

There were great crowds at the gate as Hector entered, but farther in, the streets were deserted, for the people were all on the walls. It was not the custom of Hecuba, however, to sit watching the battle, so that Hector turned his steps to the upper end of the town, where the vast columns of Priam's palace glistened white in the sun. Although Hecuba was gray and withered by now, and the rims of her watery eyes were red from much sorrow, she never sat idle. Hector found her busy directing the work of the women in her house. At his request she sent these out through the city to bid all women come to the temples with gifts. She herself went to her carved chest and took out a robe for Athene so thickly embroidered with silver and gold that it shone like a star.

Hector turned away, leaving to his mother the detail of the processions. His melancholy mood was upon him and brought forebodings that made him seek his own house. It seemed to him that the gods would not grant him many more chances to see his wife.

Andromache was out on the walls, said the servants, and Hector turned silently back through the streets to the gate. Long before he reached it, Andromache came racing to meet him with fluttering garments. Behind, her little boy's nurse was jogging along with the child in her arms.

Hector gazed at the infant, smiling sadly, and said nothing. His wife, fresh from beholding the battle, could not control herself, but clung to his arm and appealed to him with tears in her eyes.

"Hector," she implored, "stay at home for a little. Must you fight every day? Already my father and brothers have been killed, and my mother, whom Achilles set free, died of grief shortly after. Now you must be father and brothers to me, and all that I have. Take pity on me for a little, since without you I do not know how to live."

"I do not forget you, Andromache," answered Hector, looking down at her gently. "Yet if I shrank from the battle, I should be put to shame before all the women of Troy. I was born to be a warrior and must fight as my nature bids me. Yet, dear wife, do not think I am foolish enough not to know that Troy will be taken. My anguish is not for the Trojans when I think of that day, nor for my mother, nor Priam, nor my brothers, but for you. You must live out your life as a slave somewhere in Greece and hear men mock at you because you once loved me. May I be buried deep, deep in the earth where I cannot hear the sound of your crying."

He turned from her to put out his arms for the baby. The boy, however, did not recognize his father in his helmet and set up a cry. Andromache laughed through her tears as Hector put down his helmet, took up his son, and blessed him. "May you be a comfort to your mother," he said, "and a more fortunate warrior than I."

He gave the boy back to his wife, who smiled tearfully on him, and blamed himself bitterly for sharing with her the sad thoughts of his heart. "Remember," he said, "that no man can kill me before the hour of my death, which the Fates fixed at the time I was born. Even though I play the coward, that date can never be altered. Go home now and sit down to your loom. Work is better than watching."

He stooped to pick up his helmet and turned to the gate. Andromache led the way homeward, struggling vainly with her tears.

4

A Night Adventure

IT was night, and the Trojans had not returned home, but lay encamped on the open plain. The defeated Greeks, huddled inside their camp, could hear the pipes and singing of their triumphant enemies, who were drinking to Hector and a speedy end to the war.

In fulfillment of his promise to Thetis, Zeus had given victory to the Trojans. Agamemnon had been forced to implore the help of Achilles and to offer him a part of his kingdom in addition to the return of Briseis. Achilles, however, would not be moved.

"His anger is beyond all reason," said Odysseus, who had been the king's ambassador. "Your seizure of Briseis is only one cause of his burning resentment. He complains that though he has done most of the fighting, he has always been slighted, and he takes no account of the fact that other kings are older and wiser than he."

"I have injured him," admitted Agamemnon, "but by nursing his fury while we face utter defeat, he has put himself in the wrong. What shall we do when the day breaks and the Trojans attack us in our camp?"

"We cannot wait here until day," replied Odysseus. "We must do some desperate deed that will give heart to our men. Let me take Diomede and steal into the Trojan lines. Two men might pass through their sentries and cause confusion, or at least gain news."

Agamemnon nodded. "If any man can help us, you are he. I have not forgotten the ambush you set by the Trojan gates this last winter, crawling out with a few volunteers to lie in the snow and the marsh by the river bed half the night long. I wonder you did not die of the cold."

Odysseus laughed. "I almost did," he admitted, "for the others had taken thick cloaks, whereas I trusted in my hardiness and had nothing but the leather jacket I wore instead of armor for better concealment. In desperation at last I made up a message to be sent back to camp, and asked for a runner to take it. He, of course, left his cloak behind to make better speed, and by so doing he saved my life, though not in the way he expected."

"I believe you would come back safely from inside the very gates of Troy," declared Agamemnon with a smile.

"Diomede and I will return tonight, never fear. See, the fires have died down in the Trojan camp, but out on the right there are torches and the sounds of much movement. Something is happening about which we should find out before dawn."

As the bustle in the Trojan camp died to silence, two figures slipped quietly out of the rows of Greek huts, passed the sentries, and vanished into the dark.

When night fell the victorious Trojans had halted where they were on the edge of the plain. Hector was raging like a lion whose prey had escaped him. "Let the men build fires where they are," he commanded, "while food is brought out from the city. When they have eaten and drunk and are rested, we shall fall on the Greek camp in spite of the darkness."

"Hector, in defeat you are as firm as a rock, but in victory you are too hasty," declared young Aeneas, his cousin, who was wise beyond his years. "There is a palisade and a trench around the Greek ships, and we do not know the entrances. Moreover, Achilles will never let us burn the ships, but will fall on us with his fresh men when we are inside the stockade and will trap us there in the dark."

"If we take no risks," retorted Hector, "we shall lose our opportunity. Look at the lights and confusion in the Greek camp ahead of us. I believe that they are launching their ships and will make off unpunished while we wait here for day."

"Send out a scout to make sure before you risk the whole army."

"Very well," replied Hector unwillingly. "If any man dares go alone, I will do so. Who will risk his life for his country in her hour of need?"

"I will," cried a thin, dark man from the back of his audience. "I will go if you offer a reward."

"Dolon, the Wolf!" cried Hector. "You are well named for one who does deeds of daring in the night time. What reward do you seek? Gold? The life of an enemy? Some Greek king for your slave?"

"Kings make poor slaves," said Dolon sourly, "and dead men bring no profit. Nor do I need gold, since my father is rich and I am his only son."

"Choose what you wish."

"Give me the horses of Achilles," said he eagerly, "the undying horses that the King of the Sea gave to Peleus for a wedding gift. They are white as the foam on the waters and run swiftly as the wind. To possess them I will risk my life."

"You ask a great prize," said Hector soberly, "but if you can bring back news, you will have earned it."

"I am not called 'The Wolf' for nothing," boasted Dolon. "I shall wrap myself in a wolfskin with its head thrown over mine and crawl on the ground past the sentries, who will think I am a wolf or stray dog. Fear nothing for me. I shall return with Odysseus' head at my belt perhaps, or even Diomede's."

"Such heads are not easily come by," answered Hector, smiling. He raised his voice suddenly. "Who interrupts our council?" he demanded. "What man is here?"

"It is a shepherd from the foothills of Ida," cried a voice. "He brings news of a mighty army marching to our aid."

"Let him come forward," demanded Hector. "Now, man, what is this tale?"

"There was a great noise in the thickets," stammered he, "and we thought it was the Greeks, but it is not. They speak Thracian."

"Did you see them?"

"I saw a tall man who gleamed like a god in a chariot of gold. His horses were white as the snow, and they bore on their foreheads Gorgons' heads shaped out of gold with tinkling bells set around them. There were long lines of chariots behind him, and spearmen, and archers, and slingers. It was an endless host."

"It is Rhesus, the Thracian," cried Hector. "He comes in the nick of time, for with his help victory is certain. He is a great hero, and a goddess was his mother. How far away is he?"

"Not far," answered the shepherd. "I came over the hills where his men could not follow, but they are marching quickly and will be here before long."

"I must go welcome them and guide them," cried Hector. "They shall camp to the right of our army and join with us in the onslaught at dawn. Farewell, Dolon. Good luck to your errand. We need even more than before to learn what may be afoot."

The plain between the two armies lay dark and silent. Here and there deep patches of blackness marked bushes in whose shadows an unwary walker might trip over the bodies of men, since the dead of the last day's fighting lay scattered over the plain. Odysseus and Diomede heard someone ahead of them stumble heavily and curse as he did so. Dolon was taking no special pains to be quiet, since the Greek outposts were far out of earshot.

"Lie down and let the man pass," whispered Odysseus.

"Then we can chase him into our sentries if he is too quick for us."

The two flung themselves down by the side of the path, arms spread wide and bodies twisted like the dead men they had seen. Dolon passed them without a glance, whistling a little between his teeth to keep up his courage. The two Greeks watched him pass before they scrambled to their feet and made after him.

Dolon halted and turned, for he supposed his pursuers must be messengers from the Trojan camp, and in spite of his boasting, he was not unwilling to be recalled. It was not until the men were almost upon him that he saw their weapons gleam. With a sudden cry he fled wildly, attempting to dodge them and regain his own lines.

It was unfortunate for Dolon that both his pursuers were famous for their running. Try as he would, he found himself driven towards the Greek sentry posts. Presently a spear flashed over his shoulder and stuck quivering in the ground in front of him. He stopped, trembling, and the two were upon him, gripping him roughly by the arms.

Dolon's knees gave way beneath him, and he collapsed in his captors' hands. "Take me alive," gasped he imploringly. "My father is rich and will pay any ransom."

"Talk first," said Odysseus sternly, "and bargain afterwards. Who sent you and what are you doing?"

Dolon was shivering all over, and words poured out of him almost too fast to be understood. "I will tell you anything you want, and my father will pay ransom. Hector sent me to see if the Greeks were planning flight in the dark. I did not

want to come, but he promised me the white horses of Achilles
if I brought news."

Odysseus laughed shortly. "You are hardly the man for
those horses," he said. "Achilles himself finds them difficult
to master, and he is a stranger to fear. But now tell me where
Hector sleeps and whether there are guards on watch around
him."

"Yes, there are sentries," stammered he. "I cannot tell
where Hector lies, indeed I cannot."

"It were better for you if you had known," said Diomede
threateningly, lifting his sword.

With a great bound Dolon jerked himself half free and fell
on his knees on the grass. "Spare me! Spare me!" he implored. "Hector left to greet Rhesus, the Thracian, and guide
him to the right of our lines."

"Who is this Rhesus?"

"He is a great king with snow-white horses, and chariot and
armor of gold. I saw him come in as I was making myself
ready. He was a huge man who shone like the golden Apollo.
His men were all travel-stained and weary, but he looked like
a god."

"On the right, you say," mused Odysseus. "If his men are
weary, they may not set a good watch. It would be a great
deed to slay this Rhesus and carry off his horses, for without
a leader, his men will go home."

"I will give you the watchword," babbled Dolon. "It is
'Phoebus.' You can tie me here until you come back. I will
make no noise."

"Indeed you will not," said Diomede grimly, lifting his

sword. Dolon put up his hands with a gasp, but was too late. The weapon hit him where the neck joined the shoulder, and he fell in the dust. Diomede stooped to gather up the wolfskin. "We will return this to Hector," said he. "They will need it perhaps when they next send out a spy."

The Thracian men, trusting in Hector's assurance of victory, had posted no sentries. They lay on the ground in orderly rows, each man by his horses. In the middle slept Rhesus, his golden armor piled at his feet and the gleaming chariot a little to one side. His horses were unharnessed, but tied with stout leather thongs to the chariot rail.

"These are twins to the horses of Achilles," whispered Odysseus in awe. "I did not know that any other hero on earth owned such creatures."

"You and I will own them tonight," answered Diomede. "Let me fall on the king and raise confusion about him, while you loosen the horses and drive them out of the throng."

He drew his sword and ran lightly through the ranks of the sleepers. Raising his weapon over the king, he struck. There was a groan, and the charioteer, who slept by his master, leaped up with a shout. All around in the darkness men jumped to their feet, seized weapons, and hit out blindly. Over the body of the king a terrible tumult arose.

Meanwhile Odysseus was struggling with the thongs that tied the frightened horses, for he dared not cut them loose, lest he have nothing with which to control the beasts. Fortunately for him men thought him the charioteer, who lay dying beside his master. The horses were leaping and plunging as he wrenched at the knots he could not see in the dark.

A torch lit up the scene and silhouetted Odysseus. With a fearful yell the crowd surged towards him, just as the thongs parted to a final, desperate heave. There was no time to reach for the whip, which stood in its socket in the chariot. Odysseus flung himself on the back of the nearest horse, snatched his bow from his back, and brought it down over the animal's haunches.

The horse neighed wildly and leaped into the crowd, dragging his teammate with him. People scattered, and Diomede, breaking hastily loose from his enemies, caught the horse by the mane. Odysseus seized him and hauled him up in front of himself. Two on one horse, with the other beast thundering beside them, they raced off into the dark.

Next morning the Thracian men set off sorrowfully for their home. Strange horses drew the bright golden chariot, and the body of Rhesus was not with them. His goddess mother had carried it away and laid it in a cave, where he might sleep for evermore, glorious as in life. Over his body the nymphs made lament for the sorrows of an immortal mother who had borne a child that must die.

5

The Death of Patroclus

WHEN the dawn goddess arose and brought light, Zeus sent out fierce Discord to stand by the ships and cry aloud in a terrible voice, that the hearts of the fighters might be strengthened for war. Agamemnon summoned his host, while on the high ground in the center of the plain the Trojans gathered about Hector, who shone in bronze like a star. Like a pack of wolves the Greeks rushed from their huts to clash together with their enemies on the edge of the plain.

In the center of the battle, fierce Agamemnon slew Isos and Antiphos, two sons of Priam whom Achilles had once taken prisoner on Ida but set free for a ransom. Now Agamemnon hurled them from their chariot and stripped off their armor, for he knew who they were and wished to triumph over their father. Next Iphidamas, a son of Antenor, struck at the king with a spear, but Agamemnon caught the weapon with his hand and jerked furiously. As Iphidamas stumbled forward, still holding the spear haft, Agamemnon smote him on the neck with his sword.

Iphidamas' brother, mad with fury at his loss, now thrust sideways at Agamemnon through the press and pierced his arm. As the Trojan stooped to pick up his brother, Agamemnon stabbed fiercely at him under his shield, so that he fell on the corpse of Iphidamas and died.

Blood spurted from the wound of King Agamemnon, and he called for help to his charioteer, who was hovering on the edge of the battle. When Hector saw the king depart for the ships in his chariot, he cried aloud to encourage his men and rushed against Diomede, who was covering the king's retreat. A spear struck the Trojan full on the helmet, knocking him backward, half stunned. Before he could recover, an arrow from Paris' bow had wounded Diomede, forcing him also to retire from the battle.

Odysseus now stood alone in the center of the line, hemmed in like a wild boar who is baited by huntsmen and hounds. Five men he slew, but the spear of the sixth pierced right through his shield and bright breastplate and tore into his side. Odysseus shouted terribly in anger, while the Trojan turned to escape, dismayed at what he had done. With his full strength Odysseus hurled his spear after the man and hit him full between the shoulders, stretching him face down in the dust.

When they saw the blood stream from the side of Odysseus, all the Trojans crowded fiercely about him, and the hero lifted his voice in a desperate call for help. At that, Menelaus and Ajax rushed forward. Ajax held back the throng with his gigantic strength, while Menelaus helped Odysseus out of the battle.

Meanwhile Hector, who had departed from the center, was spreading havoc far off on the left by the banks of Skamander, where Nestor and his young son, Antilochus, were leading the Greek host. Here Machaon was wounded, a hero whose life was most precious to the heroes, since he was more skilled in medicine than any in the host. Nestor himself took Machaon on his chariot to drive him back to the ships.

Achilles was standing by the stern of his black ship, listening to the din of the battle. In his heart he had repented of his anger since the time that Odysseus had offered him terms in the name of King Agamemnon. Nevertheless, his pride held him back even now while the fighting was moving steadily nearer. He made no movement to help, but he turned to Patroclus, his dearest friend, who had come with him from Greece, and whom he loved better than life.

"Go and ask old Nestor who is wounded," said he anxiously. "It seemed like Machaon, though I could not see his face." Patroclus needed no urging, but shot past the ships like an arrow in search of old Nestor.

Achilles leaned back against his ship and looked at his men. Today they were not playing with javelins or quoits, but sat each in the door of his hut, silent and clad in full armor. The battle had reached the palisade and the trench. Trojans were pouring through the gateways and over the wall like the sea. Ahead of them rushed Hector, shouting to his men to leave the huts and the plunder and make for the ships.

Behind him came Helenus, Deiphobus, Aeneas, and Sarpedon, the leader of the Trojans' allies.

In front of the ships the desperate Greeks made a wall of shields, behind which the slingers of Ajax the less shot thick and fast into the Trojan throng. These came on, however, like a great storm of wind and broke into the ranks, man against man, until many heroes fell in the dust. At last the Greeks fell back from the foremast ships, except for Ajax the giant. Hector laid his hand on the prow of the nearest, which was that of Protesilaus, who had been slain long ago at the landing.

"Bring torches," he shouted. "Throw fire on it."

Men rushed forward with flaming sticks, even as Ajax leaped up on the deck with a great pike in his hands and stabbed fiercely down on its attackers. The Greeks rallied again. Some jumped up by Ajax with axes, and hatchets, and great double-pointed spears. Now, however, the Trojan slingers and javelin throwers made havoc among the men exposed on the decks. Presently Ajax gave ground to the oarsmen's bench in the middle of the ship, which was protected by bulwarks. He still fought furiously from thence, but smoke poured from the unguarded bows.

From the far end of the beach Achilles watched the fire grow with increasing disquiet. Patroclus came running back from the huts to appeal to him. "Diomede, Odysseus, and Agamemnon are wounded," cried he. "Ajax alone steadies the line. One ship is burning already, and soon the whole mass will follow. Without ships no man will escape to Greece alive."

There was a silence for a moment.

"The gray, cold sea was your mother, not Thetis," said Patroclus reproachfully. "Have you no more pity than rock?"

"No man can be angry forever," said Achilles heavily. "Although I myself have sworn to defend nothing but my own ships, you may lead my men into battle so that their fresh strength may turn the tide. I will lend you my armor, for if the Trojans think I am with you, they will fall back in dismay. Drive the enemy from the camp, but return after that and do not pursue them over the plain. Because of my quarrel with Agamemnon, I would not have the Trojans brought to utter defeat."

The battle for the ships was decided in an instant when the yelling horde of the Myrmidons took the Trojans suddenly in the flank. In front of them raced Patroclus, drawn by Achilles' white horses and wearing the star-studded breastplate and the helmet of the hero himself. With a cry of dismay the Trojans scattered, and many of them were cut off by the wall and the ditch over which they had leaped so eagerly. Patroclus pursued these among the huts and the ships, while other Greeks threw water on the half burned vessel of Protesilaus.

The Trojans soon rallied around Hector and Sarpedon, but Patroclus at the head of the Greeks rushed on them like a roaring fire. Now the heart of Zeus himself high in heaven was dismayed, for Sarpedon was his own son, born to him by a mortal princess. Even Zeus, however, would not interfere with the laws of the Fates, and Sarpedon fell to the spear of

Patroclus as an oak falls to the shipwright's axes out on the hills. Thereupon the allies of the Trojans fled in dismay at the death of their leader, and the forces of Hector followed headlong over the plain.

The battle for the ships was won, and the camp was safe, but Patroclus, disobeying the commands of Achilles, rode after the Trojans, stabbing and slaying far out over the plain. All the way back from the camp to the city the ground was scattered with corpses, for not until they were under the gates could Hector rally his men.

At last the Trojans stood firm and stopped their pursuers, even driving them back a little way. Hector now bade his charioteer lay the lash to his horses, and he tore right through the ranks of the fighters against the chariot of Patroclus. The latter, leaping to the ground with his spear in his left hand, seized a sharp stone that he hurled full at Hector's charioteer, striking him dead to the earth. Hector sprang down with a shout to bestride his friend's corpse, but Patroclus also darted forward, hoping to strip off the armor and wear it in triumph. Hector seized his comrade by the head, and Patroclus grasped him by the foot, while over his body Greeks and Trojans joined madly in battle.

A roar arose from the Trojans like the sound of a storm at sea. Patroclus gave ground, while Hector leaped over his friend's body and stabbed with all his force. With a great crash Patroclus fell. Hector looked down on him, crying, "Patroclus, fool that you were to think that you could bring my bloodstained armor to the tents of Achilles! You shall never go home to the ships to tell him who is the better man."

"Boast over me now," answered Patroclus faintly. "When Achilles hears you have slain me, you will not live long."

"Who knows?" cried Hector exulting. "These are the days of my glory, and perhaps Achilles himself will fall to my spear."

The soul of Patroclus left his body and fled wailing, while Hector bent to strip him of his armor, and over him the battle was joined more fiercely than before.

6

The Death of Hector

FROM the green caves under the sea, Thetis arose to comfort her son, but in vain, since all her magical powers could not restore him Patroclus. "In my anger against King Agamemnon," groaned Achilles, "I have sent out my friend alone to his death. What is Briseis compared to Patroclus, whose very body I cannot now rescue, unarmed as I am?"

"Alas, my son," said the goddess, clasping him in her arms, "do not kill yourself with grief for a mortal man whose end was appointed by the Fates when he was born."

"I do not care whether I live or die, since my anger and pride have brought death on my dearest friend. My only hope is revenge."

Tears sprang to the eyes of the goddess for her son, who was at once her joy and her sorrow. "At least stay out of the battle today while I go to Olympus and beg the lame smith, Hephaistos himself, to make you new armor in place of that which Hector has stripped from Patroclus. Tomorrow you may go forth to war."

"I must look now," cried he, starting up suddenly. "Perhaps at this very moment Hector is bearing off the body of Patroclus in triumph." He rushed toward the gateway in the wall, while the goddess sped up through the clouds to Olympus, where the house of Hephaistos shone with hammered silver and gold.

Achilles stood by the edge of the moat, unarmored, but huge as a giant, looking out at the battle on the plain. Three times he cried aloud in his grief and his rage, while the light of the setting sun behind him outlined his figure with fire. So terrible was he to the Trojans that they shrank back in dismay, relinquishing the body of Patroclus, which was now buried under men and broken spears.

As the battle paused, the sun plunged under the horizon. The baffled Trojans, retreating to their position of the night before, took counsel. "We must go back to the city," cried Polydamas, "while we have the chance. Tomorrow Achilles will fall raging upon us and scatter us like leaves."

"Go back?" cried Hector. "I say, no. Today we have stormed into the camp, fired a ship, and killed or wounded the greater part of the chieftains. Are you all afraid of one man? If so, I will face him alone, for I stand at a height of glory from which no man shall cast me down."

"Very well," answered Polydamas gloomily, "but the blood

of those who fall tomorrow at the hands of Achilles will be on your head."

During this while, the Greeks were making a bier for the body of Patroclus, and when the women had washed and anointed him, they laid him upon it, as handsome as he had been during life. The other heroes then scattered to their tents to rest, but Achilles mourned all night long, sleepless from rage and grief.

That same night in his palace on Olympus, Hephaistos was toiling over armor of bronze inlaid with silver and gold. He made first a great shield covered with pictures. There was a city at war upon it, and a city at peace. Men were breaking ground with a plow, and at the ends of their furrows boys were waiting with cups of wine to refresh them. Reapers were cutting wheat with sharp sickles, while boys behind them gathered it up and gave it to the binders. Men and women were bringing home the grapes in plaited baskets. Youths and maidens were dancing, their hands upon one another's wrists. All these pictures and more were on the shield of Achilles, together with which the god made a breastplate brighter than a flame of fire. Next he fashioned greaves of pliant metal, and a massive helmet crested with gold. Dawn approached as he gave the glistening armor to Thetis, who darted down from the peaks of Olympus like a falling star.

Men awoke and were summoned to an assembly, in which Agamemnon once more offered Briseis and great treasures to Achilles if he would put his anger aside.

"Keep the girl or return her as you wish," said Achilles

indifferently, looking at him with red eyes and pale, terrible face. "Who is she that two kings should quarrel for her, a captive and a slave? Forget her, and let us arm for battle. I burn for revenge."

"I wronged you, and I will return the girl and give treasure besides," answered Agamemnon with decision. "When we have eaten, we will go out to battle."

"Eat if you must, but eat quickly. I have no need of food."

Soon the Greeks poured out of their huts in their glittering armor, thick as snowflakes hovering in the winter air. Far overhead Athene shouted aloud, while opposite her Ares, terrible as a black storm, shook his vast spear. Zeus thundered from heaven until the mountains quivered and far below the dark halls of the dead trembled with the shock. Achilles rushed out to war like a wounded lion, driven on by his pain and his fury to kill or die.

First he fell upon Aeneas, whose last hour would have come, had not the gods snatched him away in mist, for he was destined to survive the sack of his city and to found a new race of Trojans who should rule over the world. Achilles, thus foiled, leaped forward again, and men gave way before him, since to stand in his path was death.

In front of him by chance ran a boy, little more than a child. He was Priam's youngest and dearest son, whom the old man had forbidden to enter the battle. The lad, however, was daring and would run up behind the fighters to throw his light spear, trusting in his swiftness to escape before he could be caught. As the warriors now parted before the onset of Achilles, this boy was exposed for a moment full in the slayer's path. Before this time Achilles had spared many a lad and let him go for a ransom, but now he had no pity left. He hurled his heavy javelin, heard the boy's shrill cry as he fell, and rushed on like fire through a forest, destroying as he came.

Achilles drove the Trojans back to the banks of yellow Skamander, where a portion of them were hemmed in by a bend of the river and took to the water in search of escape. Leaping down the steep bank, sword in hand, he slew until the reddened stream was choked with the bodies of the dead. One young man climbed back up the bank, but too late, for the destroyer saw him. The youth dropped his weapon and fell at his enemy's feet. "Spare me!" he cried. "I am Lykaon, whom you caught once before upon Ida and sold into slavery over the sea. I was found at last and bought back at a great price by my father. Twelve days ago I reached Troy. Only twelve days! Have pity on me!"

"Fool!" said Achilles, raising his sword with grim purpose. "Do you think there is mercy left in my heart for a brother of Hector?" He struck, and the young man fell back down the bank to be swept away by the eddying stream.

At last the waters were choked with the dead, and the river god himself lifted up his voice from the depths, crying to Achilles to cease. He, however, slew on until the river in rage burst its banks and roared down upon him, seeking to sweep him away. Achilles grasped at a tree and struggled painfully out of the torrent. He turned toward Troy to pursue the main body of Trojans, who were in flight across the plain.

Old Priam, from the tower by the gateway, called to the guards to fling the gates wide and hold them open as long as they dared. Soon the entry was crowded with chariots and men racing for safety, while as yet Achilles was still far off chasing stragglers over the plain. In confusion none noticed that one man had leaped from his chariot and rushed out again through the gateway. Priam saw him first as he turned to the wall again and looked out. Alone in the plain stood Hector, spear in hand, awaiting Achilles.

Priam leaned out over the wall and called to his son. "Come back, Hector! If you perish, what hope is left for me and for Troy? Remember my age and my sorrows, and spare me this worst blow of all."

The wind sweeping over the battlements blew the sound of the old man's cry away. If his son heard, he did not answer, for he was half mad with shame and grief because his rashness had exposed the Trojans to disaster. He remembered how he had promised to face Achilles himself, and the words of Polydamas' answer still rung in his ears: "The blood of those who fall at the hands of Achilles will be on your head."

The huge and dazzling figure of Achilles was racing for his enemy. Defeat had crushed the exultation of the Trojan hero, so that once more he saw clearly and knew that his death was at hand. It was easier to face death in battle than to wait for it calmly. "Suppose I put off my shield and my helmet, meet Achilles unarmed, and fall at his knees. I can promise him Helen and all the wealth of our city in ransom, since the elders will carry out what I command."

Thus he thought to himself for a moment, but the answer

came quickly. "Achilles would slay me, unarmed like a woman, and in death I should be put to shame." As though the very thought had unnerved him, he turned to run back to safety where the darts of the Trojans from the wall could cover him. Achilles, however, who was now close upon him, cut sideways across his path and drove him outward from the wall.

Now Hector fled round the walls of Troy with Achilles after him. Past the station of the watchmen they went, past the wagon track, the great fig tree, and the pools of eddying Skamander where the women washed their clothes. None dared come out from the city to help, and no Greek rushed to the aid of Achilles, for he had motioned them all to stand aside. Three times around the city the two raced for the life of Hector. Mighty was he who fled, but the pursuer was greater far.

At last when Hector saw there was no escape, he turned on his enemy. Achilles also halted, and in the pause the Trojan spoke. "Achilles, if I have the fortune to kill you, I will give back your body to the Greeks for burial, and do you do the same by mine."

"You are mad to talk of bargains to me," said Achilles, glaring furiously upon him. "Does the sheep make terms with the wolf?" He raised his arm and hurled his great spear. Hector crouched so that the weapon flew over his shoulder. He threw in his turn and hit the shield of Achilles, but the spear rebounded from the armor made by a god. Hector drew his sword and leaped forward desperately to come to close quarters, but Achilles met him with a fierce thrust in the neck between the breastplate and the helmet. Hector fell with a crash in the dust.

"Hector," exulted Achilles, "when you were killing Patro-clus, you thought yourself safe because I was not there. Now dogs and birds shall devour you, while Patroclus lies buried in state."

"Give back my body to my father," murmured Hector faintly. "I beg and implore you to let me be buried so that my spirit may go down to the land of the blessed dead."

"Dog!" cried Achilles, glorying in his revenge, "Priam shall not buy back your body if he offer your weight in gold. Beasts shall devour you unburied, and your spirit shall wander for ages without end."

"Savage that you are!" gasped Hector. "Beware the anger of the gods. It is not long before Paris and Phoebus Apollo shall slay you on the threshold of the Skaian Gate."

After this prophecy Hector's limbs relaxed as the shadow of death came over him. His soul fled forth from his body, wailing its lost vigor and youth.

Achilles looked down on the corpse. Revenge was short, and now it was over, but it had not restored him Patroclus. He needed more vengeance. Rapidly he stripped the corpse of its armor and tied it by the feet to his chariot. He drove round Troy, dragging Hector in the dust before the eyes of the dead man's parents and wife, who stood on the walls.

Even so, Hector's death brought no consolation. In the green caves under the water, Thetis wept all night long to hear her son groaning and calling upon the spirit of his friend. Briseis was regained but Patroclus, who was far more

beloved, was lost to him utterly He could not accept this, but at last he said to himself, "I will at least give Patroclus a funeral such as no hero has had hitherto." With that thought he was comforted a little. "I shall be at peace when that is done," said he.

7

Funeral Games

TWO days were spent by the Greeks over the burial of Patroclus. First they piled up great logs for the burning and brought out the body in procession to lay it on top. Each man put a lock of his hair on the dead man's bier for remembrance, while Achilles placed treasures at his feet for him to take down into the land of the dead. All day the Greeks were busy with sacrifices and prayers to the gods until evening came, when Achilles kindled the fire. The huge pyre burned all night long, while Achilles, standing in the red firelight, drew wine from a golden bowl and poured it on the earth, calling again and again on the spirit of Patroclus.

When at last all was burned to gray ashes, the Myrmidons heaped up a great mound as a memorial to their companion, and Achilles sent criers through the camp to proclaim games in Patroclus' honor.

The people came out from their huts and gathered about the prizes that Achilles had brought out for the chariot race. Five heroes were contending in this, and Achilles set out a prize for each, so that none might go away without a memorial. Men marked out a course to a withered stump with two white stones by its base, around which the chariots were to swing and return to their starting place.

The five heroes lifted up their whips and rushed forward, side by side in a whirlwind of dust. The light, springless chariots shook, rocked, or bounded into the air, while the riders balanced as best they might, feet well apart, whip in one hand, and reins in the other. Had not the floors of the chariots been made of woven straps, which gave somewhat under their riders, one or other of the heroes would surely have been thrown out and broken his neck. As it was, the chariots rattled and crashed, and the drivers swayed madly while they shouted aloud and laid on the lash.

Eumelos shot out ahead with Diomede so close behind him that the front hooves of his horses seemed about to mount Eumelos' car. Suddenly the chariot of Eumelos hit a rock, bounded up, and dropped back to earth with such a crash that its pole broke clear through. The horses rushed on, and Eumelos, whose hands were entangled in the reins, was dragged clear over the rail of his shattered car and over the stony ground. He got to his feet after a time and checked his horses. Meanwhile Diomede, driving with consummate skill, had avoided the crash and was already rounding the terminal post far ahead of the others.

The next pair were King Menelaus and Antilochus, the

young son of Nestor. Menelaus was slightly ahead, and Antilochus doubted whether his horses had enough speed to outrace the king. He waited, therefore, until he saw the track enter a hollow with steep banks on either side. As Menelaus approached this, Antilochus lashed up his horses until the two chariots were racing madly abreast.

"Keep back!" shouted Menelaus furiously. "Here the track is not wide enough for two."

Antilochus, who was younger and more reckless, responded by flogging his horses on with all his might. Menelaus reined back violently, and Antilochus swept past. Before the infuriated king could regain his speed, his young rival was a fair stone's throw ahead.

"Diomede is the winner," announced Achilles, advancing to greet the successful champion. "Eumelos, here, shall have a special prize for the sake of his injury and because his horses were really the swiftest. No man should feel that he does not get his deserts today. Antilochus takes second prize, and Menelaus the third."

"This is not fair," burst out Menelaus, pushing forward. "My horses are better, and Antilochus only pushed his ahead by reckless driving. He forced me to rein back in order to save his life and my own."

Antilochus looked at the angry king, reflecting that it was not wise to offend the brother of Agamemnon. He smiled a little, triumphing inwardly because he had in fact come in second. Nevertheless he said readily, "Take the second prize, King Menelaus. I am young and hasty, but I know it is not for me to contend with my elders."

"I will do so," replied Menelaus, still offended. "Another time be less ready to play tricks on men who are better than you."

Antilochus now took the third prize with a good grace, and Meriones, who came in last, was awarded the fourth.

Achilles took up the fifth prize, a two-handled urn that now stood unclaimed, and turned toward Nestor. "Old man," said he, "the day is past when you could share in these sports, though once you were famous. I would not have you go away, however, without some memorial of the burying of Patroclus."

"You speak well," answered the gratified old man, wagging his beard with approval. "I was indeed famous in times long gone by when no man could match me in wrestling or running. Now I thank you for this fair gift in memory of Patroclus. If I were but younger, I would challenge you all, for there were better men in those days."

Achilles listened with respect to the old man's harmless vanity, for it was true that few at his age could still go out to war. At this point, however, the prizes were being brought out for the boxing. Achilles announced that he would give a mule to the first man, and to his opponent a two-handled cup.

None of the great heroes volunteered for the boxing, which was a brutal sport, the hands of the contestants being bound with straps studded with metal. Two men stood up, but only one claimed his own prize after the contest. The other was carried off the field, and his friends went up to fetch him the two-handled cup.

Odysseus now prepared to wrestle with Ajax, who at first sight seemed easily the stronger, for he was taller by more than a head. Odysseus, however, had great shoulders and powerful arms, though his legs were short. For a while the two heroes swayed back and forth while their backs creaked with the strain and sweat poured from them in streams. At last Ajax put forth his great strength and lifted his enemy, hoping to dash him to the ground. Odysseus swiftly hit him behind the knee and twisted around to fall on his chest as he collapsed.

The first fall thus went to Odysseus, who now in his turn tried to lift Ajax, but could not. The giant swayed a little, slightly off balance. With a sudden thrust, Odysseus crooked his knee behind his opponent's, bringing him once more to the ground.

"This is a victory of skill over strength," said the heroes as Odysseus came forward to take away his prize, while Ajax stood sullenly by.

"Who will run in the foot race?" demanded Achilles quickly, because he saw that Ajax was much moved and could scarcely conceal his resentment.

At Achilles' words there was a slight pause, for he himself was by far the swiftest runner in the host. Soon, however, the other Ajax, Oileus' son, stepped forward. After him Odysseus and young Antilochus volunteered to try for the prize. Of these Ajax ran the fastest, but by very little, since Odysseus trod right in his footprints before the dust had settled back on the ground. Just in front of the goal Ajax slipped and fell headlong, for Athene wished to honor Odysseus, who was always dear to her.

"It is easy to see that the gods prefer older men," commented Antilochus smiling as he took the third prize. "Ajax Oileus is older than I, while Odysseus is of an earlier generation altogether, though few but Achilles can rival him in speed."

Agamemnon now arose to cast the javelin, and against him was set Meriones, a brave charioteer. When Achilles saw how unequal was the rank of the contestants, he interposed, wishing no awkwardness to arise upon that day. "King Agamemnon," said he, "we all know that you excel in this sport. Take the first prize without a contest, and let me give Meriones the second, if he is willing." Both champions gladly agreed to avoid a trial of skill, while the bystanders praised Achilles for his ready tact.

As the games broke up, the heroes spoke much of the noble funeral Achilles had made for his comrade. All went back to their huts contented, except for Achilles. Bitter sorrow still gnawed at his heart, for neither vengeance nor the honors he had paid to his friend had reconciled him to his loss. Twice he started up from his bed and went out to roam wildly by the seashore and listen to the moaning of the waves. When dawn came, he yoked the horses to his chariot and savagely dragged Hector's body round and round Patroclus' tomb. Even this brought him no comfort. He left Hector lying in the dust and went wearily back to his hut.

8

The Ransom

SWIFT Iris, darting down like a ray of light from Olympus, came to Priam, who was sitting in the courtyard of his palace mourning for his son. "Get up, King Priam, and be of good courage," said she, "for Zeus has sent me. Go out into the camp of the Greeks and buy back the body of Hector. Fierce Achilles shall do you no harm, for the gods will watch over you."

The old man cast off the dark cloak enwrapping him and turned to his astonished sons, who were sitting in a circle about him silently respecting his grief. "Bind a wicker cart to its framework, harness it with mules, and bid my servant Idaios be ready to drive it. Make me ready also a chariot for myself. With my own ears just now I heard the command of Zeus."

Priam went in out of the sunlight to his cool, dark house, which resounded with the wailing of women for Hector.

Around the walls of his chamber stood great chests that held beautiful garments, jewels, cups, bars of gold, and many other things of great price.

"Why are you taking out your treasures?" asked his wife wearily, finding him there. "Surely you cannot have need of them at this time of sorrow."

"I am going out to ransom the body of our son from Achilles," he declared.

"Are you out of your mind?" she cried shrilly.

"The gods have promised me protection," he answered, and left her wringing her hands.

Dusk had fallen before the mule cart was loaded and the old man and his servant were ready to drive out of the town. The anxious watchers from the city lost sight of them in the darkness, but Zeus, who saw all things from Olympus, watched them strike out across the plain.

"Go down and guide them," said he, turning to Hermes. "Bring them safe to Achilles through the midst of the enemy's camp."

Hermes bound on his golden, winged sandals that carried him like the wind, and came swiftly to Troy from Olympus, running lightly over the sea. Here he changed himself to the shape of a very young prince with the first down of manhood still on his chin.

"Where are you going, old man?" said he kindly, stepping out to meet Priam from behind a tall grave mound that rose on the plain. "You are very near the camp of your enemies and will soon run into danger, dark though the night has become. I am one of the Myrmidons, a squire of Achilles, but

I will guide you into safety in memory of my father, who is old and resembles you."

"Young squire of Achilles," said the old man desperately, encouraged by the friendly tone of the god, "tell me the truth. Does Hector's body still lie in the dirt by the tents of the Myrmidons?"

"It lies by the tomb of Patroclus, round which Achilles daily drags it, hoping vainly to comfort himself for the loss of his friend."

Priam took forth a cup of great value and pressed it on Hermes. "Take this gift," said he, "if you will guide me to the hut of Achilles."

The seeming squire drew back with contempt. "I do not need to be bribed," he said haughtily. "I will go with you because you are old and for courtesy's sake."

The god leaped into the chariot and drove it toward the trench, in front of which the Greek sentries sat cooking their supper. Priam shrank back behind his young guide as they approached the firelight, but to his astonishment, though the pot boiled on the fire, the men lay about it fast asleep. Hermes, who had enchanted their eyes, smiled gently and drove through the camp, in which he had charmed even the dogs into unconsciousness.

The hut of Achilles had a great courtyard all about it and was fenced in by a high palisade. Hermes unbarred the great gate and drove quietly in. Priam, alighting stiffly from the chariot, walked over to the door of the hut.

Achilles sat alone by a little table with two squires busy in attendance, backs to the doorway. In a moment Priam had crossed the floor and fallen on the ground before the knees of Achilles, while he kissed the terrible hands that had slain so many of his sons.

"Achilles," he implored, "think of your own father, who is as old and lonely as I. Yet while he struggles desperately in his unruly kingdom far away, he still has hope that his great son will return to his aid. I once had fifty sons, but the greater part are dead, and now Hector, the best of them all, will never come back to me or to my country in our need. Have pity and at least let me buy back his body for burial. I must be the first man on earth who has gone so far as to kiss the hands of the slayer of so many sons."

Sorrow welled up again in the heart of Achilles, but at the piteous sight of old Priam all bitterness left him at last. He moved the old man gently aside and covered his face. Both wept, Priam for his son, and Achilles for his lonely old father, and for dead Patroclus.

"Get up, old man," said Achilles at last very kindly. "Our griefs are only the common lot of mankind, after all. My father Peleus was a hero once and the richest and happiest of kings. What use was his fortune, however, when he begot an only son who was fated to die very young? Even while I live, I am no comfort or help to my father, but am fighting here very far from my country, making misery for you and your children. You, too, were once happy and powerful, but now battle and death have swept all your good fortune away."

The old man looked at him without moving. "Get up,"

said Achilles again. "What use is all our lamentation?" he added, sighing heavily. "We cannot raise those we love from the dead."

"Hector lies on the bare ground," Priam persisted. "Why should not I?"

"I will fetch you your son," said Achilles, rising to go out and summon his men.

When he had delivered the body of Hector to his followers to be washed and wrapped in fine garments before it was laid on the mule cart of Priam, Achilles turned to the grave of Patroclus and spoke to the spirit of the dead.

"Patroclus," cried he, "do not be angry if I give back Hector's body to his father. We have had revenge, but it is no use to us at all. It is better for your memory's sake that I take fitting ransom from Priam." The dark grave made no answer, but Achilles felt the consent of his friend deep in his heart.

Priam sat huddled in a chair by the hearth trembling from head to foot, overcome by the reaction from his former courage, which had been born of despair. Achilles looked down at the old, wrinkled face and the furrows from the corners of the eyes that marked the track of tears. "Let us eat and drink quietly together," said he kindly, seeing that the old man was incapable of rising. "Afterward you shall sleep a little before you take Hector home. I have not closed my own eyes since the death of Patroclus, but now at last my heart is at peace."

PART 4

THE CLOSE
OF THE WAR

1

The Queen of the Amazons

MEN were running to lift down their weapons from the wall and hastily putting on their armor. Once more the rumbling of chariots and the neighing of horses were heard in the streets of Troy. For many days after the death of Hector, the leaderless Trojans had despaired of ever driving the Greeks into the sea. Deiphobus and Helenus, now the greatest of the princes, were hardly friends with one another, though they both resented the rivalry of Aeneas, since he was not one of Priam's sons. The peace party, headed by Polydamas and Antenor, was openly seeking support from the people, even though no one could suggest any terms the victorious Greeks would be likely to accept. Discouraged and frightened, the

Trojans had huddled inside the walls of their city, where they might soon have been closely beseiged if Achilles had not held back the Greeks in order to give Priam a breathing space for celebrating Hector's funeral.

Twelve days were now over, and contrary to all expectations, the Trojans were going out again to war. In the midst of doubting and despair a new champion had come to their aid. This was Penthesilea, queen of the Amazons, a nation of warrior women. She was even now riding across the great square on her way from the palace of Priam to the Skaian Gate amid the cheers of the men and women who thronged the streets. Only white-faced Andromache watched doubtfully, half hidden behind the colonnade of Hector's house. "Hector was a warrior," she said softly, "but this is a young girl as slender as I. How can she be a match for Achilles, as she boasts? She does not really understand war."

For a moment the townspeople had forgotten Hector, absorbed in this new wonder which had appeared to save them. Penthesilea sat astride a fiery white horse, and from the waving crest of her helmet to the sandals on her feet she glittered with gold. Slender though she was, she easily carried a round shield with two javelins fastened behind it, while her right hand grasped a huge spear. From a broad belt across her shoulders hung a sword in a scabbard of ivory and silver. She appeared to wear her heavy armor and to manage her horse with the lightness and grace of the huntress, Artemis. Behind her rode a guard of Amazons, two and two. All were young, but none rivaled the queen, whose helmet was pushed back on her forehead, uncovering her lovely face, delicately flushed with excitement as she raised her spear in answer to the Trojan cheers.

The great gates were swinging open, and soon the shouting crowd of Trojans was swarming out to battle. Penthesilea set her horse to a gallop, and with a wild cry she and her guards tore across the plain, followed by the rocking chariots of the princes and the rabble of light-armed troops racing behind them on foot.

Scouts rushed into the camp of the Greeks to find the army unbelieving and unprepared. "They will not dare to challenge us seriously," said Achilles to Ajax, who stood with him by the mound of Patroclus, making sacrifices to the spirit of the dead. "They have been too terribly beaten to be dangerous. There is no need to interrupt our rites."

Elsewhere in the camp men rushed for their arms and poured out onto the plain confusedly, each when he was ready. Penthesilea, with her maidens behind her, fell on them like the goddess of war.

The first to meet the onset of the Amazons were the men of Protesilaus, led by Podarces, the dead hero's brother. Six of these fell to the queen's spear and were trampled beneath the red hooves of her plunging horse. Meantime Clonie, the maiden on her right hand, laid low Menippus, Podarces' greatest friend. At that Podarces himself, with a great shout, aimed his spear at Clonie and hurled her dying from her horse. Penthesilea, turning on him like a fury, stabbed him through the arm. The blood spurted forth like a fountain, and Podarces died in his friends' arms as he was being carried out of the battle.

At the loss of their leader, the men facing the Amazons turned to flee with cries of dismay. They were, however, caught between the Amazons and the Greek forces still pushing out to the battle, so that many of them died from a thrust in the back or turned to face their enemies unprotected, since they had thrown away their shields. In vain did Diomede leap forward and take the life of a maiden as the group rode thundering past. In vain did fresh forces run up to the rescue. The main body of Trojans was up with the Amazons by now, and their impetus was not to be stayed. The Greeks were rolled back to their camp with the great, white horse of Penthesilea racing at the head of the pursuit.

As the roar of battle rolled down on the Greek camp, Achilles and Ajax, roused by the noise, issued from the gate like two lions and charged on the advancing foes. The Greeks rallied with them and fell on the Amazons, who were soon entangled in a mass of men, among whom their desperate valor did fearful execution. Achilles and Ajax cut through the throng towards Penthesilea, killing as they went. She, seizing one of her javelins, hurled it at Achilles but saw it shatter to fragments against the shield a god had made. Swift as a flash she plucked forth the second and aimed it at Ajax, but in her haste her aim was poor. The weapon glanced off his silver greave, and the giant laughed at her as he plunged past to fall on the Trojans behind her.

Achilles flung up his spear and hit Penthesilea full in the breast. She rocked in the saddle, fumbling blindly for her sword. Long before she could draw it, however, the hero stabbed upward at the plunging horse with such force that the spear went right through beast and rider. Both fell with a crash to earth.

The Trojans turned and fled desperately, their short-lived courage entirely gone. Achilles, however, did not join the pursuit. "Foolish woman," said he, stooping over the dead queen's body. "Who persuaded you that you were strong enough to fight with men?"

He wrenched off her helmet roughly, and then stopped with it in his hand, staring. The queen lay lovely and fresh as a wild rose on the bloodstained field. Her beautiful lips were parted a little, as though she still breathed, and her soft hair had fallen about her shoulders, shining in the sun. Achilles straightened up slowly, still looking at her. "It is a pity that one so fair should die so young," he said. "Had I been fated to go home with the Myrmidons and be king in my father's room, what better queen could I have set by my side than this girl with the gallantry of a warrior and the beauty of a nymph? I could have loved her, but instead I have killed her. The price of glory is high indeed, for it is always bought by death."

2

The Last Fight of Achilles

BRIGHT Dawn, daughter of the mists of Night, flung wide the gates of heaven for the chariot of the sun. Her rosy light shone palely on this gray morning on which her son, Memnon, lord of Ethiopia, was going out to war. Long ago when Priam was still a youth, his brother, Tithonus, had been loved by the dawn goddess, who carried him away to dwell with her in her many-colored house forever. Memnon, their child, now ruled over all the dark peoples of the distant East at the edge of the world itself. So far was his kingdom from Troy that only in the tenth year could he bring help to his uncle. Now at last he had arrived with a mighty army to hearten the discouraged Trojans with the thought that they too had a hero who was goddess-born.

Far under the sullen sea, Thetis sat silent in the midst of her maidens. The wisdom that was hers from her father made her aware of death standing over Achilles, and she dreaded the gigantic son of the goddess of dawn.

Dust swirled over the plain of Troy as the dark hosts of Ethiopia rushed like a whirlwind into the fight. The sound of their wild yells ran echoing over the ridges of Ida, while the distant halls of Olympus heard the crash as rank met rank.

Swarthy Memnon was a giant matched only by Ajax, but rivaling Achilles in furious speed. The great spear he wielded was so huge that its point alone was half the length of a man, yet Memnon swung it in one hand as though it had been a reed. He fell upon Nestor's men, who stood in his path, like a lion on a flock of sheep.

Men dropped to right and left of the warrior till he walked over corpses and the parched earth was wet with blood. Young Antilochus, furious at the overthrow of his followers, stepped boldly out in the path of the giant to throw his spear. Memnon did not wait to receive the weapon on his shield, but leaped forward two men's length at a single bound, stabbing as he came He landed with such dreadful force that his spear pierced shield and breastplate and stood a handsbreadth out behind the young man's back. Antilochus fell dead without a cry.

Old Nestor, maddened to desperation by the loss of his eldest and most beloved son, snatched the whip from his charioteer to lash his horses into the fray.

"Keep back, old fool," shouted Memnon. "It is not for you to fight with such as I."

The old man leaned forward in his chariot and cast his spear with a quivering hand. Memnon laughed as it fell far short, and he turned aside into the press of the battle. Nestor wavered for a moment, near to tears for his dead child and for his own feebleness. "Let Achilles avenge my son," he said at last, turning away, "for he has always loved him well."

Now the pale goddess of dawn sighed heavily, and the little winds that attended her chariot shivered with fear. Thetis covered her face, lest her straining eyes behold the death of her son. Rank on rank the immortal gods looked down from their thrones of cloud as the sons of two goddesses met like twin thunderbolts upon the plain of Troy.

The swords of the champions flashed like lightning as they rained down blows more swiftly than the eye could follow them. Twice they closed shield to shield, and their tossing crests of horsehair mingled as they wrestled, each stabbing for the other's throat. Achilles seized from the earth a deep-rooted boundary stone that had marked the limit of the plow-land in far-off, happier times. No other Greek but Ajax could have lifted such a weight and hurled it on his opponent like a stone sped from a sling. The immortal temper of Memnon's shield withstood the impact, and behind it the great giant stood immovable. For a moment Achilles too paused in wonder. Then with a roar the champions leaped together once more, and fire flew from their smitten helmets.

Dust arose and settled on the fighters. Sweat caked it on their faces. Dark splashes of blood from the struggle around them flecked their limbs. About them, the battle raged like a storm at sea, while maddened horses trampled on the bodies of the slain. However, there was a clear space about these giants in spite of the press, for none dared intervene between the heroes sprung from the goddess of dawn and the silver-footed nymph of the sea.

Wind swept aside the dust of battle, and the immortals high in the air cried aloud with a sound of thunder, for by Memnon stood black Fate, and by Achilles a glory like a god. With a mighty thrust Achilles' sword sped clear through Memnon's body and the giant fell like a great tree, his armor clanging about him in the dust.

Dawn covered her bright face in cloud while shining Achilles bent to strip off the armor from the dead. The little winds with soft sighing slid gently down to earth in silver mist, and lifting the corpse of Memnon, bore it away.

Achilles shouted with triumph as he leaped on the Ethiopians, and scattered them howling before him, sweeping with them the Trojan forces, who had trusted in their might. Men threw down their shields in panic, or climbed on their chariots and fled. But though they ran with desperation, Achilles, clad in full armor, was swifter far. Soon the gates of Troy were flung open, but so great was the press of fugitives struggling for safety that no man could close them again. A great cry arose from the walls, for in the midst of the mass raced Achilles, and now he stood and slew in the space between the open gates.

"Troy is taken," cried the women from the walls, while the children who stood about them shrieked with panic, and the old men shouted vainly to the helpless guards of the gate. Troy would have been taken indeed, were it not for Phoebus Apollo, who had loved and watched over the city since its founding long ago.

Swift as a ray of sunlight, Apollo left his seat in the clouds and stood in the courtyard by Paris in the likeness of a young man. "Will you not shoot for Troy's sake?" said he, giving him an arrow.

Paris stood on the steps of a palace far out of the throng, for he had been among the first to turn tail. He fitted the arrow to his bow with trembling hands and shot over the heads of his people at the gleaming figure in the gate.

The arrow was hastily aimed, and its force was soon spent. It dropped at the feet of Achilles, and would have plunged harmlessly into the earth, had not the hero turned suddenly to ward off a blow aimed at his back. As he did so, the arrow of the coward pierced him in the heel where Thetis had held him long ago when she dipped his body into the Styx.

Achilles staggered for a moment as the fiery poison of the god burned through his veins. Elsewhere in his body the magic of the Styx would have protected him from the venom, if not from the wound. He recovered, made one more thrust at an enemy, then dropped his sword and collapsed in the dust.

With a great shout of triumph, the Trojans rallied, while the Greeks rushed forward to rescue the body of the hero from between the enemy's gates. Once again these were jammed open as men struggled to turn and rush back into the battle. Soon the space between them was trampled and dark with blood. The body of Achilles lay beneath the feet of the fighters, face-down upon the earth.

3

The Armor of Achilles

A TERRIBLE wailing surged out of the depths of the sea, as though the waves were washing the sound up against the coasts of Troy. Out in the bay the waters rolled apart, revealing a company of women in the midst of whom rode Thetis on the crest of a wave that broke into foam about her silvery feet. Little ripples of light danced around her and shimmered on the water over which she passed. So fair was she, in spite of her sorrow, that the men on the beach stared at her in awe as she flung herself down by the bier on which they had placed her son.

Thetis lifted the bright head of Achilles and pillowed it upon her arm. "My son, my darling, why were you born to this end?" lamented she. "Why did Zeus force me to marry a mortal and bear him a child, though I am the daughter of the ancient sea? Even in his boyhood I had no joy in my son because he could not live with me in the green caves of my father. When he became the greatest of heroes and my pride, I could not even comfort his grief. Now he, who has conquered Dawn's son, lies slain by a coward. Alas for Dawn! She too knows what it is for an immortal to be mother of a man who must die."

The goddess fell on the body of her son and kissed it, while her nymphs took up a dirge. The Greeks stood by in silence, awe-stricken by the sight of gods and the lovely sound of their song. The sun went down and the moon came up, but all night long men were bewitched by the music of the immortals, while tears ran down their cheeks for the death of a man who was beautiful and short-lived as the spring. How long they were entranced, they did not know, but afterward they seemed to have passed in a dream through many nights and days.

At last the dirge was done, and Thetis bade men light the fire to burn Achilles as Patroclus had been. This they did, and the ashes of the two comrades were laid together.

Next Thetis caused the spoils of Achilles to be brought forth from his hut and given as prizes for the funeral games in his honor. There was a golden cup that had been the greatest treasure of Andromache's father in Thebe before Achilles took that town. Two silver bowls had been the price of Lykaon when Achilles sold him in Lemnos over the sea. There were the arms of Hector, of Memnon, and of Troilus, whom Achilles had cut down in the flower of his youth. Cattle came from raids on Mount Ida, and slaves from countless cities, together with many talents of gold. All these things were given as a memorial to the dead hero, but Thetis kept back until the last, the greatest treasure of all.

"Here lies the armor of Achilles, which the immortal Hephaistos made for him," said she. "There is nothing like it upon earth, and it shall be worn by the man whom the Greeks judge the greatest hero now that my son is dead."

"I claim this prize as my due," stated Ajax proudly. "You all know that I am the strongest fighter left in the host. It was I who defended the ships when Achilles sat in his tent and the rest of you were wounded or turned tail. For this service alone I have earned the armor, even if I had not proved my valor a thousand times in the years that we have been at Troy."

"The merits of Ajax are great, but mine are yet greater," said Odysseus. Ajax turned on him with a haughty stare, but the king continued calmly. "I am not as strong as Ajax but I have been of far more service to the host. My persuasions brought you to Aulis. My advice has guided you in trouble. I was your ambassador to Troy. More than this, I too am a fighter, not so great as Ajax in the melee, but far more dangerous, because more cunning. It was I who set the ambush by the gates of Troy, and I who went with Diomede by night to kill Rhesus before he had struck a single blow on behalf of his friends."

"Such tricks are not fighting!" cried Ajax furiously. "How dare this smooth ambassador and spinner of words claim to rank above me? I shall kill him for this insult!"

The Greeks looked at one another in consternation. Old

Nestor put a hand on Agamemnon's arm and muttered advice in his ear. "We cannot choose between two such heroes," said Agamemnon turning to the throng, "but Nestor reminds me that we have some judges among us who have no interest but to be fair. Let us call out our Trojan captives and ask them which of the two they fear most."

"There should be no question," said Ajax haughtily. "You all know I could break this plausible cheat in two."

Odysseus smiled in silence, while the other chiefs applauded Agamemnon's words with great relief, for they had feared that a terrible quarrel would disrupt the host. The Trojan captives were speedily assembled and the question put to them. They answered readily.

"Our men fear Ajax in battle," said they, "but the whole city dreads Odysseus like the spirit of death itself. He is the evil genius of Troy."

"You shall repent the judgment," cried Ajax hotly. "I am the greater fighter, as all admit, and I will have my right."

"The award was fairly made," said Agamemnon. Ajax could not trust himself to answer, but turned and stalked off to his hut.

Odysseus took the arms of Achilles rejoicing, though he could not wear them, for Achilles had been far taller than he. Still, he laid them in his hut and was accepted as the greatest hero in the host, while Ajax brooded over revenge.

Little Tecmessa, who was Ajax's captive and whom he had promised to make his wife, sat watching her lord with wide, frightened eyes as he grasped his sword and muttered to himself. Once or twice she ventured a timid question, but got no answer. Teucer, who was always kind to her, had gone on a raid, taking the greater part of Ajax's men. Tecmessa gave her little boy to his nurse and whispered to the woman to keep him out of sight, for she was frightened. She lit a lamp and sat down beside her lord, wishing the night was past.

To Ajax, brooding over his defeat, it seemed impossible to go home and face his father after such a disgrace. Old Telamon was a hard, ambitious man whose pride in his son was greater than his love. If Ajax came home without the armor of Achilles, Telamon would regard him as a coward who had not been willing to stand up for his right. The bare thought of this was intolerable to the hero. He started up, sword in hand, and went out into the dark.

It was Ajax's purpose to fall upon Odysseus and Agamemnon in their tents and slay them, together with such of their men as came to their help. What happened next, he did not care. There would have been great slaughter in the host that night had it not been for Pallas Athene, who watched over Odysseus. She now touched the mind of Ajax with madness, so that his glaring eyes passed by the huts of his enemies and fixed themselves upon the great, fenced space in which the cattle and sheep that fed the host were penned.

The herdsmen were peacefully sleeping when the huge figure of the madman charged upon them, sword in hand. Those that awoke in time fled screaming, terrified out of their wits by the great figure bearing down on them in the

moonlight, his shining armor flecked by dark stains of blood. Ajax did not pursue them, but fell upon the helpless sheep, and slew until the pen was heaped with bodies. Seizing upon two huge rams, whom he took for Agamemnon and Odysseus, he bound them tightly, slung them over his shoulders, and carried them off in triumph before the servants could return with help.

Tecmessa, waiting in Ajax's hut, was appalled to see him return red to the elbows and stained from head to foot with blood. He was muttering to himself and did not see her as he slung the two rams down in a corner of the hut.

"My lord —" said she faintly.

Ajax made her no answer. He put his hands to his hips and rocked back and forth in front of the two rams, gloating. "Who is the greatest hero now?" said he, bursting into a roar of laughter so loud and meaningless that the frightened girl could not fail to see that he was completely out of his mind.

Tecmessa crouched in a corner while Ajax delivered a furious tirade to his captives, abusing them and threatening them with every kind of dreadful death. It was soon plain to her what must have happened, but the knowledge was no use, for she dared not call for help, lest her mad lord fall on his own servants or run amuck through the host.

At last the gray light of morning fell through the open door, and she heard Ajax falter, then stop in the middle of what he was saying. Quickly she looked up. The man was staring at the creatures in front of him as though he could not believe his eyes. "He sees them as they really are," thought she. "In another minute he will realize what he has done."

Ajax staggered away and sat down with his head in his hands, uttering a deep, long groan, the first that Tecmessa had ever heard from him.

The girl crept to the door and went out to get help from the servants, for she saw that Ajax was beside himself with shame and rage, and feared lest he do himself an injury. She knew well that his proud spirit would never endure the mockery that this night's work would bring on him.

Outside, the camp was in an uproar. Ajax had been recognized in the moonlight by one of the herdsmen, who had now told his tale. Wild stories were going around the camp that Ajax was dangerous and must be put out of the way like a mad dog. Teucer, coming back with his men from the raid, was mobbed by a crowd shouting that he was brother to a madman who had attempted to murder the leaders of the host. Agamemnon was summoning an armed guard to surround Ajax in his hut.

Quickly Tecmessa hastened to Teucer and told him all that she knew. "You must come immediately," gasped she, "or he will kill himself. I know he cannot endure the shame of such a deed."

Teucer ran for the hut with Tecmessa at his elbow and his men crowding behind. He motioned to them to stand back while he pulled aside the curtain and went in. After a second he reappeared at the entrance. "Ajax has gone!" said he.

"Scatter and look for him," implored Tecmessa.

"Down by the seashore," added Teucer. "He would not go among the tents."

Tecmessa was already halfway to the shore, running wildly. They saw her climb one of the sand dunes and fling herself down on the other side of it with a desolate cry. They found her lying across the body of Ajax, which lay stretched in the hollow with a sword in its heart.

"How could you leave me, my lord?" sobbed Tecmessa. "I was your wife, and my boy is your heir. Now that you are dead, your proud father will never own me because I have been a slave. I shall be only a servant to him, and your boy will be brought up in slavery with his mother."

"I will look after you, Tecmessa," said Teucer kindly, laying his hand on her shoulder. "I too was the son of a captive, though my mother was by birth a princess. I know what your fate has been, and I will acknowledge your boy as my brother's heir. To my father I am but a useful servant for Ajax. Perhaps he will not even receive me if I go back home and tell him I am alive, but my brother is dead. If that be so, many will follow me into exile, for Ajax's men love me. Then you and your son shall be with us, and somewhere we will make a new home."

He lifted the girl gently from the body and guided her home, while his men took up the great hero and followed slowly.

"Ajax has raised his hand against his overlord, with whom he had sworn to keep faith," said Agamemnon indignantly when he heard all the tale. "Such a man is accursed and

deserves not to be buried at all, but to wander desolate for
ever on the mud banks of the Styx, cast out from heaven and
earth."

"I beat **Ajax** fairly," said Odysseus, "and he attempted my
life in return. However, death pays off all scores. He was a
great hero, and we shall not see another fighter like him on
earth again."

4

Pyrrhus

AFTER the deaths of Achilles and Ajax, the Trojans took heart, the more especially as another champion had come to their rescue. This was Eurypylus, the grandson of Heracles, and nephew to Priam through his mother. Machaon was slain by this hero, leaving his men leaderless, since his brother, who was much younger and had looked to him as to a father, was prostrated with grief.

"Such sorrow is unmanly," declared Nestor in a council of the heroes. "I too am plunged in mourning for the loss of my son, Antilochus, yet I can still lead my men into battle where they are needed for the protection of us all."

"Ajax would have been a match for Heracles' grandson," put in Menelaus spitefully. "Odysseus has been judged the greater hero, but what help has he for us now?"

Agamemnon glanced anxiously at Odysseus, but the hero

showed no sign of taking offence. "I was never as strong as Ajax," he admitted readily, "but I have some advice to offer that may well turn the tide. Eurypylus himself would not be a menace if our men fought with better heart. As it is, though Ajax's men follow Teucer, the Myrmidons are leaderless since the death of Achilles and have aided us but little, despite the fact they are the strongest group in the host. Did you ever hear that Achilles had a son?"

"A son?"

"He was secretly wedded in Scyros when I found him disguised among the princesses there, and he had a child, well grown and forward for his age, who should be nearly a man by now."

"Surely his mother will never allow the boy to leave her before he is even grown," said Agamemnon doubtfully.

"Will a son of Achilles be ruled by a woman? Besides, the old king, his grandfather, will realize that the boy must come to take command of the Myrmidons or lose his inheritance. Let me go over to Scyros, where I am known and my words will carry much weight. I will offer the armor of Achilles to the boy in proof that I accept him as the hero's son."

"I will give him Hermione, my only child, in marriage if he will come," cried Menelaus. "She is a bride of such rank that he must know we acknowledge him as Achilles' heir."

"Go then with the gods' blessing," said old Calchas, the prophet. "This very night it was revealed to me that we shall not take Troy until a son of Achilles is here."

The swiftest of the black ships on the beach was pulled down to the water's edge and twenty picked rowers took their places within her. Men stepped the stout mast and hoisted the sail. Soon they were beyond the bay and striking out over the sea toward the distant island of Scyros, which was one of the stopping places on the long route to Greece.

There was a good harbor at Scyros, and rough quays had been constructed on the seashore opposite the town. Odysseus, however, bade his men pull in to a sandy beach seemingly deserted, for he thought it best to come in unnoticed and gain news.

In a little meadow outside the walls, a young man was hurling the javelin. As it flashed through the air, he started after it with the speed of a deer and seized it by the handle while it was still quivering from its impact into the earth.

"That is he," said Odysseus confidently. "Achilles could catch the javelin before its point touched the ground, and this youth is almost master of the feat. In any case, there can hardly be two such giants in one town."

The youth, turning round with his weapon in his hand, saw the strangers and halted. "Who are you?" he called cheerfully. "And what brings you here?"

"We are friends of Achilles, your father," answered Odysseus. "What is your name?"

"I am called Pyrrhus," answered he, "and I am indeed Achilles' son, though I had supposed that my birth was unknown."

"Not to me," answered the hero, smiling, "for I am Odysseus, and I have come here to fetch you to the war, as I came for your father. You are very like him, I think, and may prove yourself to be as great as he."

The young man was indeed almost as tall as his father, though somewhat less handsome. His hair was pale yellow, and his eyes very light blue, while his features were thinner and sharper than Achilles' had been. "He looks colder than his father," thought Odysseus, "and he may be more cruel in war." He fell in beside the young man and walked into the town with him, answering all manner of questions about the glory of Achilles and the war at Troy.

Deidamia, as Agamemnon had foretold, dissolved into tears, declaring that her child was too young to lead an army or to fight with the champions of Troy. "Is it not enough that you took my husband from me?" she wailed.

"I am a hero's son, and I shall go," declared Pyrrhus shortly.

"He must go," said the old king, "if he is to be known as the son of Achilles and succeed to Peleus' kingdom. Be wise, my daughter, and dry your tears, for these things have to be."

Deidamia threw herself on her son's breast, twining her arms around him. He kissed her, though without much tenderness, and put her away. "My mother is foolish sometimes, though she knows that my heart is set on war," said he, taking his place by Odysseus in the prow of the ship, while his servants crowded into the waist.

"You shall wear your father's armor against Heracles' grandson," said Odysseus. "I give it you freely, for you look as though you were made for it, as I never was."

The young man smiled happily on Odysseus, charmed by his generous words, while the rowers glanced at one another in amusement, because they had listened to Odysseus before.

"Your young master is eager for battle," said one in a low voice to the nearest of Pyrrhus' servants. "He could hardly say farewell to his mother, and he never looks back at the land that has been his home."

"He is proud and he is harsh," replied the servant. "Nevertheless, he is already a warrior such as we in Scyros have never seen."

5

The Bow of Heracles

THE arrival of Pyrrhus to lead the Myrmidons discomforted the Trojans greatly. They were driven back once more, while their champion, the grandson of Heracles, was slain by the son of Achilles. Nevertheless, the Greeks were still unable to storm Troy or to besiege it and cut off its supplies. In despair Agamemnon bade Calchas consult the omens to find out why it was that the gods still denied the capture of Troy.

"Troy will not be taken until the Greeks bring the bow of Heracles against it," reported he.

"The bow of Heracles!" repeated the chieftains, looking at one another in dismay.

The bow of Heracles and its quiverful of arrows had been poisoned in the blood of the dreadful Hydra. They were left by the hero to his comrade, Philoctetes, who had set out with the host from Aulis toward Troy.

It had chanced that the fleet of the Greeks came to anchor by a little island on which there was a sacred grove and an altar. There Calchas revealed to them that the host must be purified by sacred rites. Philoctetes, however, rashly approaching the altar without due reverence, was stung in the foot by a serpent issuing from beneath it.

The wound proved quite incurable, and the whole fleet was disturbed by the sick man's cries of pain. It seemed impossible to take him farther, seeing that the ships were so cramped that it was necessary to go ashore to cook and sleep. Meanwhile the purification rites could not be performed except in total silence. Once more some chiefs began to murmur that the gods were against them, and that it would be best to sail home.

At last by the advice of Odysseus, Agamemnon resolved to abandon Philoctetes on an uninhabited island nearby. When the sick man had fallen into an uneasy sleep, men rowed him over and set him down by the mouth of a cave, with a few rags to bind up his wound, a bag of provisions, and the famous bow and arrows close by his hand. There they had left him, then performed their rites and departed for Troy, never doubting that death had overtaken him within a few days.

If Agamemnon's conscience was ever troubled that he had deserted the wretched man in his need, ambition readily quieted it. Odysseus was far too wise to engage in an action he would ever regret. For his part he was convinced one man's death was better than the misery that would result if the expedition failed and Agamemnon's overlordship were weakened throughout Greece. Nevertheless, even Odysseus looked somewhat startled at Calchas' words.

"The bow of Heracles!" he repeated, wondering. "So Philoctetes did not die!"

"If he lives now on that deserted island, he will rather burn the bow and perish himself than come to our aid," said Agamemnon, frowning gloomily. The silence of the other chieftains signified agreement.

"What the gods have commanded, they will fulfill," declared Odysseus hardily. "Give me a ship, and I will bring the bow to Troy."

The heroes stared in amazement at that resourceful man for whom no task ever seemed too great. Agamemnon fingered his beard dubiously. "Philoctetes is armed with the arrows of Heracles, from which a scratch means death," he pointed out.

"Never fear," said Odysseus smiling. "I am fated, the prophets say, to be killed by one of my own kin. Let me take Pyrrhus with me, for he was not among us when we forsook Philoctetes, so that the hero can have no grudge against him now."

Pyrrhus gladly consented to go with Odysseus, for he was completely won over to the side of the wise king who had come to fetch him in Scyros, recognized him as his father's son, and had freely given him Achilles' armor. Had not the king generously admitted that Pyrrhus was greater than he in war? The young man was flattered and charmed, yet even he began to look dubious as the plan of Odysseus was unfolded to him.

"You shall go up to the cave alone," said Odysseus, "and

tell Philoctetes your name. Say that you are going home from
Troy because you have quarreled with me, since I withheld
from you the arms of your father, which were awarded to me
by the host. Offer to take him back to Greece with you and
to help him down to your boat. Then lay your hands on the
bow of Heracles as though to carry it for him. Once you hold
this, he is at your mercy."

"Must we tell so many lies?" faltered Pyrrhus, hardly lik-
ing to differ from his admired friend. "I cannot tell lies
well," he added, blushing a little. Although he was proud, he
was honest and innocent of heart.

"We must indeed, or betray our comrades," said Odysseus
firmly. "Otherwise we could not approach him, since he is
an archer who never misses his mark."

Pyrrhus unwillingly consented, but he was thoroughly
wretched when he stood before the cave to which Odysseus
had directed him and saw the pitiful lair in which Philoctetes
had existed all these years.

For the moment the cave was empty, but traces of Philoctetes' presence were all around. There was a small heap of
firewood in one corner. In another lay his bed, a few branches
piled over with the feathers of countless birds. Near this lay
a rough wooden bowl in which some herbs were steeping in
water. A few stained rags lay beside it and, except for the
ashes of the fire, this was all.

Pyrrhus' eyes were moist with pity to think of ten years
spent in such misery. Turning around, he saw Philoctetes
crawling toward the cave, dragging his injured foot behind
him. Over his back was slung the great bow, and in one hand

he clasped the carcass of a bird, which he had evidently killed with an arrow. Pyrrhus ran to help him up and saw that the man was black from exposure and dirt, and was wasted to a skeleton. His only coverings were a few rags and the long hair straggling over his shoulders. His shoes were worn out and discarded, but one foot was clumsily bound with strips of cloth. Philoctetes' joy and gratitude were so overwhelming that Pyrrhus could hardly blurt out the story that Odysseus had prepared for him.

Philoctetes was too much excited to notice the hesitations of his companion. He poured out questions, exclaimed over the death of Ajax, who had been his friend, and sympathized fully with the supposed ill-treatment Pyrrhus had suffered at the hands of Odysseus. "That man is too wicked to die," said he vehemently. "May he live on a deserted island far from home for ten long years, as I have done by his contrivance." He gathered up his bowl of herbs, which he said somewhat relieved his pain, and thrust his bow into the hands of Pyrrhus, begging him to carry it until they reached the ship.

Pyrrhus hesitated with the bow in his hands, but the eager gratitude of Philoctetes was too much for him. He turned back in the pathway and actually held out the weapon to its owner. "Stop a moment. I have something to tell you," said he.

"Give me that bow!" Odysseus stepped into view from behind the rock whence he had been watching the success of Pyrrhus' errand.

"Odysseus!" screamed Philoctetes. "My bow!" He too made a snatch at the weapon, while Pyrrhus hastily scrambled backward, holding it out of reach of them both.

"Give me the bow," demanded Odysseus with authority. "Troy cannot be taken without it, so that for the sake of the whole Greek host, we must bring it back. Remember the honor that we have paid to you, and the glory you stand to win in war."

Pyrrhus turned hesitatingly to Philoctetes. "Will you not come with us to Troy?" asked he. "Calchas has said that if you will do so, you will be healed of your wound there. For this reason, and for the sake of the many heroes who have not wished to injure you, come with us and forget the past."

"Never!" cried Philoctetes. "Shall I forget cold, hunger, pain, loneliness, and despair? Shall I forgive the schemer whose crooked counsels condemned me to this fate? Give me my bow!"

"Follow me, and leave him," said Odysseus sharply, turning on his heel. "The gods demand the bow, not the bearer. Let him live here ten years more!"

The young man followed unwillingly, looking back at the wild, miserable figure steadying itself against a rock.

"Curses upon you!" cried Philoctetes hoarsely. "What had I done to you, son of Achilles, that you should come to me with lies and steal my bow with a promise to take me home to Greece?"

"Take back your bow," cried Pyrrhus suddenly, running toward him. "I am no thief or promise-breaker, and I will take you to Greece if you wish. Will you not come to Troy, however, for healing awaits you there?"

"How can I trust the kings who once betrayed me?'

"They are wiser now, and their need is desperate; without you they cannot take Troy."

"How can I forget?" began Philoctetes, and stopped suddenly, looking up as a strange shadow came between him and the sun.

On the hillside above the cave stood a vast man leaning on a huge and knotty club. Pyrrhus gaped, for though he himself was of great size, the stranger overtopped him by a head. Never had the youth seen such shoulders, such arms, or such hands as those which rested lightly on the enormous club. Philoctetes too stared astonished, for he was seeing the shape of a man who had long been dead.

"Heracles!" said he, gasping.

"Go to Troy, my comrade, and win glory," said the apparition in a deep, slow voice. "Healing awaits you, and wealth, and a joyous return to the land of your birth if you will put aside your anger against the chieftains, for such is the gods' decree."

The figure faded slowly into mist and vanished from sight, while the two heroes watched him in silence. Philoctetes took his hands from the rock against which he was leaning, and straightened himself. "Come here and lend me your shoulder," said he. "You must carry my bow to the ship, for Odysseus is waiting."

Hopping and hobbling with his arm around his companion, he passed slowly down to the beach.

6

Oenone

A ROUGH stretcher carried by four bearers passed out of the Trojan gate and struck up into Ida. The bright curls of the man who lay on it were matted with sweat, and his face was pale under its tan. He twisted and groaned now and then as the men jolted him over the rough paths seldom frequented except by the shepherds. Still, he never asked them to stop, even when they passed through a brook, and the cool water splashed around their ankles. The bearers were scarlet in the sun, and a myriad flies drove them almost to madness, yet they did not halt at the stream, but toiled panting up grassy slopes and through hot woods, or broke into a rough trot whenever the path led them downward.

Once when the track went up a set of steep rocks like gigantic stairs, they paused for a moment, panting heavily. The restless head of the sufferer lifted, and the dry lips opened to whisper, "Hurry!" The men took up their burden again and began to clamber over the hot rocks toward the belt of trees above.

They were getting far up on Mount Ida now, and looking down over the foothills they might have seen the white temple of Apollo rising from the citadel of Troy. Up here there was no sound or sight of the struggle in front of the town on the great plain running down to the sea. This was wild, peaceful country where shepherds and goatherds lived on berries and goatsmilk cheese. Even Achilles had not penetrated so far, for these people owed no allegiance to Priam and kept themselves apart from the war.

In a pocket of the hills a little stream had been collected into a pool by a rough dam of stones. Only a few yards below, it leaped out over the cliffs in a wide arc of spray and tumbled down the hills into Skamander, which carried it out to sea. Skamander was yellow with the sand washed down by many such streams, but up here the pool was clear as crystal, and the trickling brook sang like a clear bell. A grove of trees shaded its banks, and across the water was a little cavern with green bushes beside it and its entrance carpeted with yellow flowers.

"Here!" said the sufferer. "Put me down now, and get water."

One man hastened to bring a drink cupped in his palms, while the others plunged their burning faces right into the icy pool.

"Call her," said the sick man more loudly, and he lifted up his own voice to cry, "Oenone!"

"Oenone!" repeated the four in chorus, timidly at first, and then as no answer came but the echoes, more loudly until the hills were ringing, "Oenone!"

Suddenly she was there, outside the cave and looking at them across the water. She wore the shining gown he remembered, and her limbs were pale brown and her hair the rich color of chestnuts. Her lips used to smile, but they did not do so now.

"Paris!" said she sharply. "There was a time when you were a shepherd and thought a nymph good enough for your bride. Now you are a great king's son, and nothing will do but the fairest woman in the world. Where is Helen, and why are you here?"

"Oenone," said he with hoarse pleading, "Philoctetes, who carries the bow of Heracles, has come against Troy and has wounded me with an arrow, as the Fates decreed he should."

"Where is Helen?" said she again bitterly. "Is her gold-and-white beauty too delicate to bear the sight of a man in pain?"

"She cannot heal me," said he. "The prophets tell me that no one can save my life but Oenone, who loved me once."

"No one has power over Heracles' poison but me, yet why should I save you?"

"Have mercy," he said, struggling to lift himself. "I am dying in agony, and you used to love me well."

A golden-green light fell through the branches over his beautiful hair and his smooth cheeks, ruddy with fever. He smiled at her imploringly, looking lovely as he had been in the flower of his youth. Oenone took a step forward into the sunlight. "Behold me," she demanded eagerly. "Am I not as fair as Helen, after all?"

Paris opened his lips to agree with her, but he could not. "Helen," he said in dazed tones, lingering over the very sound of her name. "Helen is fairer than the dazzling sun itself."

"Then let her cure you," cried the nymph, "for I will not." She put up her hands to her face and ran sobbing into the cave.

"Take me up and go home," said Paris to his bearers. "If I must die, I will see Helen again."

The men shuffled off down the slope, more slowly now. Their lord did not hurry them, and he drew in his breath less sharply when one stumbled over a stone. Presently his blue eyes closed, though he still breathed with a hoarse, straining sound.

The sun was very low when they got off Ida, and when they called to the sentry at the gate, it was already dark. Men brought torches to light them through the gateway.

"Your master is quiet now," said one. "Did Oenone put some herb on the wound to draw out the poison, for he seems as though he is asleep."

"He is dead," cried one of the bearers sharply. "He must have died out there in the dark."

The men went in with their litter, and the guards turned back to the gate.

"So he is dead," said the one who had spoken earlier. "This will be the end of the long war."

"Not so," answered the other, "for we still have Helen."

"Ah, Helen," said his fellow with awe. "Who would not die for such a woman as she?"

"Not Paris! He went back to Oenone for healing, and it seems she cast him out."

"Would he had never been born!"

Someone knocked on the gate from without. "Let me in," said a voice. "I am the nymph, Oenone, and I bring herbs for the healing of Paris."

"Paris wants no herbs," said the guard roughly, "and without the watchword I cannot open the gate."

"I will save his life," implored she. "Go in and tell King Priam that I am here to save his son, whom I have loved for so long."

"Paris is dead," shouted he. "It is but a few minutes since the bearers brought his body in through the gate."

There was silence for a moment, and then a sobbing. The guard, peering over the wall, could see nothing, though the moon had arisen and the space by the gateway was clear.

"Go home, woodland spirit," cried he in panic, and threw down his javelin in the direction of the sound.

The noise stopped abruptly, and silence fell over Troy. Far up on Ida a wolf howled by the deserted cave.

7

The Taking of the Palladium

THE bow of Heracles had performed the task for which the gods had brought it to Troy by killing Paris, yet the war still lingered on, since Deiphobus and Helenus, rivals for the leadership of the Trojans, both aspired to marry Helen. Deiphobus, who was the greater fighter, was at last victorious, whereupon Helenus fled to Mount Ida, in fear for his life.

The Greeks, who had hoped that the death of Paris would end the long struggle, were greatly disheartened. Again it was Odysseus who gave them fresh courage by leading a party up Mount Ida to capture Helenus.

"Helenus, like his twin sister, Cassandra, has the gift of prophecy," he pointed out. "Out of jealousy of Deiphobus or in fear of his life he will tell us how we can take Troy."

"I only know that Troy cannot be taken as long as the Palladium stands on the citadel," declared Helenus, smiling slightly, for he thought it would hardly be possible for the Greeks to remove the Palladium without capturing the city first.

The Palladium was a small wooden image, hardly more than a tree trunk, roughly carved to represent a woman with a spear in her hand. It was very old and was said to have fallen from heaven in the days of Ilus, grandfather of Priam, as a symbol of the gods' special favor toward Troy. It stood in a little wooden temple of Athene in the midst of the citadel, and the priestesses who served it were among the noblest women of Troy.

The Greek chiefs looked blankly at one another, discouraged by Helenus' words. Odysseus said nothing to help them, and for some time thereafter he was not seen in the camp at all. Early next morning, however, when the Trojan gates were opened for the herdsmen to drive in cattle for slaughter, an old Greek beggar limped up to the gates of Troy.

The old man was sturdy looking, but lame and pitifully ragged. He had been dreadfully beaten, to judge by the marks on his half covered shoulders and arms, while his eyes were red as fire from weeping. His tongue, however, was ready enough, and he was soon showing off his welts to a half curious, half pitying crowd, while whining for alms and telling them his tale.

He had been one of the men of Palamedes, he said, and as such had drawn down upon himself the special anger of the crafty Odysseus. For a while after Palamedes' death, Ajax had protected him. Now, however, his enemies had driven him from his hut and reduced him to beggary, since he was too old and crippled to defend what was rightly his. He had taken to wandering through the camp, lending a hand to the stewards or the herdsmen in return for a meal, and had not been above snatching at other men's food when his need was most great. This last had been his undoing, for he had been caught by the Ithacans and hauled before Odysseus, who had had him scourged out of the camp.

"Pity a poor old man," whined he, "who fought with heroes once. My father was a friend of King Tyndareus, who trusted me with the training of his young sons, Castor and Pollux. Then I slew a man in a quarrel — for I was hot-blooded in those days — and I fled for my life to Palamedes, who made me a captain among his men."

"If you knew Castor and Pollux," said one, "their sister, Helen, will gladly give you alms. Tidings of their death have reached her, but she does not know how or when they died."

"Thank you, kind citizen," said the old man, cringing. "Will you not give something to a poor man, that Helen may see her friends are well received in Troy?"

"Helen lives in the house of Deiphobus," said the citizen calmly. "It lies by the citadel, nearest to Hector's, and any man will tell you the way. As to alms, Helen herself may reward you as you deserve."

The old man hobbled off up the street, muttering resentfully, while a little group of idlers lounged after him, curious to see the meeting between Helen and a Greek after all these years.

Helen came hurrying out into her courtyard with two maids

behind her, while the old man raised his face and fixed his clear, gray eyes on hers. Helen halted, and her cheeks went pale as marble. Her lips opened, but no sound came.

"Pity a poor old man," whined the beggar rapidly. "I bring you news of your brothers, who live, though no longer on earth. One day they feast with the gods, and the next they sleep in death. Thus each is half immortal and shares the pleasures of the blessed ones."

"Come in and tell me more," said Helen faintly. "Forgive me, old man. I think the sight of a friend of my youth has taken away my wits."

She turned back into the house with the beggar limping after her. The spectators scattered, disappointed, while in her own room behind the great hall, Helen faced the Greek alone.

"Odysseus!" said she. "How dare you come into Troy? I knew you through your disguise."

"I wooed you," said he, "and stayed long with your father, but few men here have seen me without a helmet shading my face. I came on an embassy once, but that was long ago."

"Nevertheless you are in great danger. Why are you here?"

"Perhaps to see Helen, for whose beauty many men have risked their lives."

"I am a Trojan now," said she, "and you are a spy. Why should I not cry out your name in the streets of the town?"

"Helen," said he leaning forward earnestly, "you were proud of Menelaus' wealth and power. You loved Paris. What binds you to Deiphobus?"

"What do you suppose?" answered she bitterly. "Do you

think the Trojans love me after all these years of war? I must have a protector who is powerful in Troy."

"The great Trojan champions are all dead, and the war draws to a close. What if the Greeks take Troy? Who will protect you then?"

Helen's wide blue eyes were fixed on him, and she sat very still.

"Help me now," said he urgently, "and I will tell Menelaus that your heart is turned to him, though you are kept in Troy against your will. Who knows, you may again spin your fine purple wools in Sparta and see your daughter, Hermione, once more."

"What do you want?"

"Who is the priestess in the temple of Athene?"

"Theano."

"The wife of Antenor? He has always been of the peace party and, I think, would be glad to be saved when Troy is taken, together with his sons and all his house."

"He has no hope for Troy. Of that I am sure."

"You must help me to talk with Theano, but first, how many guard the citadel, and how many the Skaian Gate at night?"

"Only two in each place, for the wall cannot be scaled, and that gate is never opened after dark."

"Very good. Now give me alms and a meal, as you might to a beggar, and send a message to Theano, that I may speak with her. Think kindly of Menelaus if you can, for I know that he loves you still."

There was a great outcry at the Skaian Gate that night

when a man cut down the two sentries, drew the bolts, and fled out into the dark. Those who ran up just too late declared that their enemy was Odysseus, for one of them had seen him clearly by the light of the torch that burned near the gate. Remembering the beggar, men now realized the truth, but they had no suspicion of Helen, since Odysseus had spent a long day begging in all the principal palaces of the town. Men were amazed at his daring, but none could suggest a reason for the deed.

"We will double the guards at the gates for the future," said Deiphobus, "and command them to examine more closely the people they admit to Troy."

This was done, but no more strangers asked to enter, and for a while the nights were peaceful as before. Odysseus was waiting for the passing of the full moon.

On the first pitch-black night since Odysseus' adventure, two men stole over the plain to the point where the walls of Troy rose highest, since at this spot they were built over a cliff where the rocks at the edge of the citadel dropped down to the plain.

"There are only two guards along this wall," whispered Odysseus. "Had not the moon been full, I could have taken the Palladium when I went into Troy. This part, they think, is too steep to be scaled, but you and I, Diomede, will climb it with a rope to help us. Get up on my shoulders and take hold where the rock is not so smooth. There is a ledge up there on which the wall is built, and you can stand on it while you let the rope down for me. Then you may mount on my shoulders again and with a leap get your hands on the edge of the wall."

He straddled his legs and stood waiting. His companion jumped on his shoulders and hoisted himself up into the dark. A stone, dislodged by his passing, bounced down the rocks and crashed to the ground. Both stiffened and stood still. After a long minute of silence, Odysseus again heard the cautious sounds of Diomede feeling his way towards the ledge in the rock above. Presently a rope came dangling through the darkness, and in another minute Odysseus stood beside his friend.

"Keep on your belly as you go over the wall," he whispered, putting his mouth to the other's ear. "Dark as it is, someone might see us against the sky."

"Where do we go?"

"The temple of Athene lies beside the great, white temple of Apollo. Theano, the priestess, has promised me that it will be unwatched tonight."

"Will she keep faith?"

"I have sworn to protect Antenor and all his house in the taking of Troy. He has always despaired of the future, and is ready to save what he can."

"I see." Diomede swung himself up again, crouched on Odysseus' shoulders, and leaped for the top of the wall. Odysseus felt for the rope, but it was not there. He heard a shuffling sound on the wall and a long, sighing groan. Someone exclaimed sharply. A weapon fell with a clatter and bounced off the wall, narrowly missing Odysseus on the ledge below.

"Diomede!" he called gently, reflecting that without the rope he must stand on the ledge till dawn.

"I came up between the guards," whispered Diomede from

above him. "Did you hear me kill them? One was actually asleep!"

"Hurry then, and let down the rope. It will be dawn in an hour."

Diomede laughed softly in the darkness. "This is no errand for two men," he whispered. "I will steal the Palladium, while you stand there and catch it when I lower it on the rope."

"This is my adventure," protested Odysseus as loudly as he dared.

"This part is mine," answered Diomede chuckling. "I am younger and lighter on my feet. Moreover, I am at the top of the wall."

Odysseus, boiling with fury at being outwitted, waited for what seemed an endless time until he heard sounds above, and the rope with the image tied to it came jerkily into reach. In another moment Diomede landed heavily beside him and drew down the rope.

Odysseus turned on his companion, but in an instant Diomede had whirled to let him see the sword in his hand.

"They say no man gets the better of Odysseus and wins," he stated grimly. "I do not know the truth of this saying, but I will go first down the rope. I shall wait for you at the bottom, and while I carry the Palladium you may walk ahead."

In the gray light of dawn Odysseus came back to the camp, while Diomede stalked behind him, the Palladium strapped to his back and the sharp sword ready in his hand.

PART 5

THE FALL OF TROY

1

The Trojan Horse

ALTHOUGH the Palladium was captured, the Greeks could not yet take Troy by storm, but caused it to be spread about that they had decided to raise the siege and go home. Meanwhile they constructed a huge wooden image of a horse, in the belly of which a dozen men could lie concealed. The most daring heroes took their places in this, while the fleet actually put to sea and made sail. Across the ocean in full view of Troy lay a little island, once prosperous but during the long war abandoned and deserted. There the Greeks beached their ship out of sight on the seaward side, while they sent men to its highest point to watch for the signal light that should summon them secretly back to Troy.

Meanwhile the gates of the city were flung open, and the

populace of Troy ran shouting over the sandy plain to explore the deserted camp. Children swung on the palisade where Ajax and Hector had once met in fierce combat, or played hide-and-seek through the lanes along which Priam had driven by night to ransom his dead son. It was the first carefree day that the boys remembered as they ran laughing down to the banks of Skamander, where Achilles had hurled Lykaon into the stream.

A crowd of elders, approaching more soberly, gathered around the great horse, doubting whether the Greeks had built it in honor of a god or to bring some last sorrow to Troy.

"Such an image must be sacred," said one. "It would be wise to build an altar near it and sacrifice to the gods who have delivered our city."

"Burn it!" cried Laocoon, the priest of Poseidon. "I do not know what this is, but I have learned to fear even gifts when they come from Greeks. Who knows, there may be men within!" He lifted his spear and hurled it with all his force at the creature's side. The weapon stuck quivering in the stout planks, while from within there echoed a hollow clang.

"Hear the sound of armed men!" cried the priest.

"Keep back!" shouted another. "The image is sacred, and such a clashing marks the anger of the gods."

The people hesitated, looking to Priam for direction, but as they did so, a cry arose from the youths on the banks of Skamander, who had found a man hiding in the rushes there. Overpowering him by sheer numbers, they bound his hands behind him and dragged him toward the group.

The pent-up hysteria of ten years seemed suddenly to explode at the sight of the stranger. A group of women rushed at him, clawing and kicking, while he ducked his head and cowered among his captors, crying out at the top of his voice.

"Kill me! Kill me, then!" he shrieked. "You can do no more than the Greeks!"

Some of the men leaped forward to his rescue, pulling back the women and thrusting them aside.

"Bring the man here," called Priam. "Let us at least learn what he has to say."

The stranger flung himself at the feet of Priam, with his hair wildly disheveled and his pale face striped with scratches and marked here and there with blood. "Let me die," he repeated wildly. "How can I live when both Greeks and Trojans cast me out?"

"What is your story?" asked Priam coldly. "Why are you left to our mercy, seeing that we have no reason to love Greeks?"

"My name is Sinon," said the spy, fixing his pale, cold eyes on Priam. "I was a friend of Palamedes, after whose death I boasted I would take vengeance on Odysseus, fool that I was. Lately since Diomede broke into the temple of Athene and laid hands upon her most sacred image, the Palladium, the Greeks have utterly lost the favor of the gods. Indeed their prophets say that they will be lucky if they come home dishonored, saving nothing but their lives. All agreed that their cause was hopeless, but for many days the wind would not even let them sail." He choked and paused for a moment.

"That last is true," said Priam thoughtfully, "but go on."

"Men began to think of the days at Aulis, and a saying ran through the host that the gods would once more demand a sacrifice. At that time I saw Odysseus talking with Calchas, and the eyes of both rested upon me. I was warned, but would not believe that the two were conspiring against my life. Men pressed Calchas to name the victim, and after he had pretended for a long time that he would not, he let himself be forced. In seeming reluctance, he chose me."

"Yet you escaped."

"Men bound me to bring me to the altar where the priest waited with his knife, but I burst the thongs holding me, and fled. For two days I have crouched in the reeds while the camp was filled with the bustle of departure. Now at last my enemies are gone, but they have left me to the Trojans, whose mercies are no tenderer. Kill me, if you wish, for I am desperate with starvation and seem to be hated by gods and men."

Sinon looked up anxiously into the face of Priam, knowing that his fate and the lives of those in the horse depended on the success of his false tale. Old Priam regarded him with pity, for he was a desperate-looking sight, shivering and covered with mud from the marsh where he had lain.

"This is a happy day for Troy," said the king, "and one on which it is fitting to show mercy. Tell us, however, what is that horse, and why have the Greeks left it here on the plain?"

Sinon had ready on the tip of his tongue the story he had to tell in order to persuade the Trojans to take the horse into the town.

"The gods bade us make a sacred image," he burst out, "and Calchas declared that if the Trojans destroyed it, ruin would fall on them. If on the other hand, they placed it in the citadel, it would protect them as the Palladium used to do. Moreover, as long as it stood in Troy, the city would increase in power until at last it would rule even over Greece.

For this reason Odysseus bade his comrades make the horse so large. 'The Trojans will never take it into the citadel, since to do so they would have to pull down part of their wall,' said he."

There was a moment's silence while the people pondered Sinon's words.

"The man lies," said Laocoon sharply. "Will you never learn that you cannot trust a Greek?"

"Perhaps he does," said Priam doubtfully, "yet if not, we may do great damage to our city by lifting our hands against the horse. Let us sacrifice to the gods who have delivered us, and in the course of our prayers, they may send us a sign."

The wise words of Priam were obeyed, and presently men brought sods to raise an altar by the seashore, while servants drove down a bull for the sacrifice, and Laocoon, Poseidon's priest, put on the sacred woolen bands of his office in order to raise his hands in prayer.

Suddenly a woman shrieked and pointed out to sea. Two serpents were coiling through the water with dreadful speed toward the land. Paralyzed with fright for a moment, the crowd watched the flat heads rear above the surface, while the flickering tongues licked greedily at air. Black drops of poison ran from their jaws, and their hissing sound was heard above the breakers rolling up the sandy beach.

The two creatures were in the shallows now, and as they touched land, the crowd scattered, screaming. The monsters paid no attention to any save those against whom they had been sent. They flung themselves on two youths, Laocoon's sons, who had lingered too long near the shore, and wrapped them in their writhing coils.

With a great cry Laocoon himself rushed to the rescue of his children, but in another minute he too was helplessly entangled, while the fierce fangs of the monsters darted at his face. Shouting vainly for help, he wrenched at the coiling bodies, striving always to free his two sons and sacrifice himself. Already he was too late. The boys were limp in the choking grip of the serpents and could do nothing to free themselves. Soon the whole strength of the fierce creatures was turned against the priest, who fell with a great scream in the midst of the writhing heap. In another moment the serpents had loosened their victims and sped back to the sea, leaving the mangled bodies behind them on the beach.

The people stared at the horrible sight in silence, sobered in the midst of their festival at the dreadful thing that had occurred.

"It is clear enough that the image is sacred," declared Priam finally, "since terrible vengeance has overtaken the man who struck at it with a spear. Let us finish our prayers to the gods, and then we will attach ropes to this image and haul it up to the citadel even if we have to make a breach in the wall to get it in."

All applauded the wisdom of Priam, save Cassandra, the king's mad daughter, in whose prophecies no one believed. Led on by the false tale of Sinon and the effect of the serpents Poseidon had sent to insure the taking of Troy, the people hauled up the horse and broke down their walls, little thinking as they tugged on the long ropes that they were dragging destruction into their town.

2

The Sack of Troy

F OR the last of many times the moon shone silently
down over the walls of Troy. Even Cassandra, the
prophetess, worn out with strange visions, slept
dreamlessly, while watchmen dozed on the benches
by the gateways, and the people, weary with rejoicing, lay
quiet in their palaces or huts. No sentries stood on the watch-
towers to see the white sails of the returning fleet spread out
over the gleaming waters of the bay.

In the dark shadow cast by Apollo's temple, Sinon was
fumbling with the secret bolts of the wooden horse. Presently
the door dropped with a slight creak. A rope followed it.
There was a muffled ringing of bronze as the fully-armed
heroes slid quickly to the ground.

"Have you lit the signal, Sinon?" whispered one.

"I held a torch over the wall and watched until one flashed
in answer from the island. Already the bay is covered with

our ships, and in half an hour the men will be at the gates of
Troy."

"You are a brave man, Sinon," murmured Odysseus. "You
have carried through a hero's deed."

"Such lies are necessary," said Pyrrhus curtly, "but it is
better to win fame in open fight. To the gates now! Kill all
the guards and open the way for our army into Troy."

Keeping in the shadows of the walls, the heroes stole
through the streets, unseen and unchallenged, while the ships
grounded on the beach and men leapt out, on fire with eagerness for the plunder of Troy.

The house of Aeneas, Anchises' son, lay at the end of a
lane behind the main group of palaces, from which it was
separated by a dark grove of trees. Aeneas, like all the rest,
had feasted late that night, and now he slept sound and long.
When at last faint screams and distant shouts awoke him, he
opened his eyes to a red glare of light that he thought for a
moment was day. Starting up in dismay, he looked out to
behold the house of Deiphobus in front of him wrapped in a
sea of flame. Menelaus, hot for vengeance, had rushed
straight for the palace of Helen's new husband, had hacked
Deiphobus to pieces, and had set fire to his hall. Even as
Aeneas watched it, the roof fell in with a mighty crash.

The Trojan hero rushed out to his courtyard, through
which terrified fugitives were already streaming from other
parts of the town. It was not clear from their confused re-
ports that all was lost, and the braver men determined at least
to sell their lives dearly. With Aeneas at their head, a little
group advanced rapidly into the shadow of the trees.

"Hurry up, men!" called a voice in Greek. "There is much fighting to be done, and this is no time to come up late from the ships!" The speaker, advancing toward the Trojans in the darkness at the head of a band of Greeks, realized too late that he was among enemies. The Trojans, leaping forward like wolves, pulled down their foes before these had recovered from their surprise.

"Put on their shields and helmets," called Coroebus, one of the Trojan band. "Wearing these, we may again be taken for Greeks and may cause confusion in the dark."

It was the work of a moment to put on the Greek armor, protected by which they spread havoc among forces twice their number as they fought their way toward the center of the town. As they burst into the great square by the citadel, around which the palaces of the princes were all ablaze, they heard a scream and turned to see Cassandra, her light hair flying, being roughly dragged out of the temple of Apollo.

Coroebus, who was to have married Cassandra, gave a great cry and rushed out into the square after her, slaughtering as he went. Aeneas' men charged behind him, but here the square was bright as day from the fires, and they were easily recognized by the Greeks, while the distant Trojans on the roof tops took them for enemies and showered them with stones. Attacked by both friends and foes, they were soon overwhelmed. Aeneas and two others finally forced their way out into a darkened alley, leaving their companions dead amid a pile of slaughtered Greeks.

Meanwhile, across the square the house of Priam was under desperate siege. Men and women tore huge beams from the roofs to hurl down upon their attackers. In the shadow of the pillars a group of defiant Trojans was slowly hacked to death in front of the great door. At last huge Pyrrhus leaped up the steps with a two-headed axe in his hand to batter an entrance into the great hall. Under his thundering blows the bronze-studded doors were burst and shattered. Pyrrhus darted in with his followers at his heels, while within the shrieks of Priam's daughters-in-law and their little children rose wildly on the air.

Queen Hecuba herself, with some of her daughters, had taken refuge on the steps of the household altar. Priam was buckling on with trembling fingers the armor he had not worn for twenty years.

"What use is there in your fighting?" cried Hecuba to him in sharp, anxious tones. "You can hardly lift your weapon, let alone strike a man. Leave that to others, and come here and sit by me."

The old man suffered himself to be dragged to the altar, thinking perhaps that his presence would be a protection to his daughters there. The shrieks from the outer rooms were growing in volume, and presently a boy burst through the doorway, running for his life with the bloodstained figure of Pyrrhus close behind.

It was Polites, one of Priam's youngest children, and a favorite among those left. A groan burst from the old man's lips, and he half stood up. At that very moment Pyrrhus struck, and the lad fell at his father's feet, pouring out his life in streams of blood.

"May the gods repay you with evil," cried the old man,

snatching up his spear. "Shame on you! Your father, Achilles, knew mercy, but you have a heart of stone." He threw the spear at Pyrrhus with all his feeble strength, but the weapon glanced easily off the warrior's shield without making a single mark.

Pyrrhus' pale eyes were standing out with fury, and his arms were red to the elbows with Trojan blood. "Go complain of me to my father among the dead!" cried he, stretching out a huge hand to grasp Priam by the long, white hair. With a quick jerk he pinned the old man against the steps of the altar and plunged his sword into his breast. Priam fell back against the queen's feet and rolled to the floor, mingling in death his blood with that of his young son.

Delayed by the siege of Priam's house, the Greeks had left the more distant palace of Aeneas still untouched. That hero hurried back from the scene of destruction in the square, convinced now that resistance was hopeless and anxious only to save his wife, Creusa, his little son, and aged father. He found these gathered in his hall, together with servants from his household and fugitives, who still poured in from other parts of the town. There was no time to be lost. Hoisting his father on his shoulders, and grasping his son by the right hand, Aeneas bade the others follow closely and set out for a gate that faced towards Ida, hoping to slip away in the dark.

The black alleys were traversed quickly, and soon the party stood in the shadow of the gate, which the Greeks, knowing this side of the city less well, had not yet occupied.

"Quick, my son! Quick!" cried old Anchises, peering over the heads of the others from his vantage point on Aeneas' shoulders. "Greeks are racing out of the square toward us. I can see the light on their shields."

"Quick!" echoed Aeneas. "Through the gate! Scatter and save yourselves! I will meet you at Demeter's Mound." Hearing shouts behind him, he set off at full speed, clutching his father's legs tight against his chest, and holding up the little boy by the hand to keep him on his feet.

When the first mad rush was over, Aeneas looked back to find himself alone. Even his wife was not behind. He felt a pang of uneasiness for her, but supposed she was with one of the servants and hastened on to the meeting place.

All were soon assembled, but Creusa was not among them. Despairing, the hero went back to the gate, but Greeks held this in possession, and his wife was not to be found. At last he retraced his steps, for day would soon break, and he knew that the lives of the others depended on his leadership.

Weary and despairing, the little band trudged into the hills, looking back from time to time at the red light their burning city cast upon the sky. Aeneas walked with his son, and the boy's presence gave him courage, since it reminded him of the words of his mother, the goddess Aphrodite. "You shall live to found a great city," she had said, "and your sons' sons shall be rulers of Asia, and of Greece, and of all parts of the world."

3

The Women

DAY dawned on the smoking ruins of Troy. A group of noble women, set apart from the other plunder to be prizes for the chieftains, huddled together in the shelter of the broken wall, waiting to learn their fates. Hecuba's white hair was blown by the wind, and her wrinkled face, which had seemed only yesterday to be carved in lines of rigid pride, was now slack and fallen with hopeless despair. Of all her children, three alone remained. Polyxena, her fairest daughter, pressed close against her, stunned by the vista of the long years of misery ahead.

Cassandra, the strange prophetess whose mad fancies had troubled the Trojans through all the years of the war, was combing her hair and singing softly to herself. King Agamemnon, smitten by the sight of her wild, unearthly beauty, had chosen her out of all the captives to be his own, swearing

that he would make her his bride in defiance of Clytemnestra, his proud wife, who waited for him in Mycenae. Cassandra, to whom for years the very name of Agamemnon had brought confused storms of madness and horror, now prepared for her fate with a smile and was calmly decking herself for her bridegroom. The despair of her mother and the sick dread of her sister were hardly even realized as she pondered on the fate she foresaw her bridal would bring to Agamemnon.

One hope remained to Hecuba. Her youngest son had been a mere child when the war broke out. At that time Priam, fearing for the fate of his city, had secretly entrusted the boy to his friend, the king of Thrace. With him he had sent a vast treasure, so that if Troy should fall, his surviving child might have means to gather the scattered people and perhaps rebuild the town.

In this boy, now a young man, lay all the queen's consolation. She did not yet know, though she was soon to learn, that on hearing of Troy's destruction, the king of Thrace would murder the lad for the sake of his treasure. No one, he believed, could call him to account for his treachery, but in this he erred. When the Greek fleet was to rest at Thrace on their homeward way, Hecuba, pretending ignorance of her son's death, would entice the king into the camp by offering to entrust him with the secret of more treasure that had been buried in Troy. The covetous king would come eagerly, and the captives, overpowering him by their numbers, would take terrible revenge.

All this lay yet in the future. Now Hecuba was able to take courage in the thought of this one son as she watched

Talthybius, the oldest of the Greek heralds, coming slowly across the browned grass toward them with a group of servants at his heels. He was a tall man with a broad, pleasant face just now twisted into unnatural sternness by the unwelcome task before him. He halted in front of the motionless queen and cleared his throat.

"The lots are drawn, Hecuba," he said awkwardly. "You are to be Odysseus' slave."

"Not Odysseus' slave!" Hecuba's hands went up to her straggling hair and clutched it, while her voice cracked weirdly. "Must I learn to bow and scrape before that dreadful man whom we in Troy hate above all other Greeks?"

"His wife, Penelope, is a gracious lady," said Talthybius kindly, "and Odysseus himself is merciful toward those who obey."

"I never thought to need the mercy of that man! However, any misery that comes must needs be brief. What of my daughters? They, poor things, are young."

The herald's hand went to his beard in hesitation, and he glanced at the servants behind him for support. "Cassandra is for Agamemnon," he said quickly. "Never fear for her. The king loves her and will make her his bride in despite of Clytemnestra, his wife."

"Ah, I know," the old queen glanced at her unseeing daughter, who sat alone, covered as with a cloak by her silvery hair. "Take her. She is crazed by this night's terrors and, I think, realizes nothing of her plight or ours."

"Yes, mother, I know it all," said the prophetess softly without moving. "I am ready. You thought me too tender for war, but I tell you that none of us shall have vengeance braver and bloodier than mine."

"I am glad at least you are willing," said the herald, looking with pity on the strange girl. "You and your sister must rise and come with me."

"Polyxena? What is in store for her?" cried the agonized mother, while the girl shuddered all over and crouched lower on the ground.

"No life of misery awaits her," replied the herald hastily.

"Some evil is planned, I am sure of it," exclaimed the queen, frightened by the man's embarrassment.

Talthybius stood irresolute for a moment, as though hesitating how to break the news. "She is to be slain as a sacrifice by the tomb of Achilles," he stated abruptly at last.

Hecuba cried aloud and clung to her daughter, but the girl now got up steadily, putting her mother away. "That is good news, mother," she said gravely. "I dreaded a life of sorrow and shame. It is better to die." She turned to the herald. "Let us go while my mother is still stunned by the news," said she.

Talthybius made no move to take her, but stood hesitating. "There is also Andromache," he stated finally.

Hecuba, hanging on her daughter's neck, paid no heed to this, but Andromache herself. who sat on the ground with her child asleep on her lap, turned white as death. "What of me?" she demanded quietly.

"Pyrrhus takes you. Have no fear, for he has heard that you are gentle and of good repute, so that already he loves you."

"A curse lies on me," she answered bitterly, "if my very virtues are to bring down on me the worst fate of all. Am I to be loved by savage Pyrrhus, whose father slew my husband and all my kin?"

"Be comforted," said Polyxena gently. "You still have Hector's child."

"As to the child — " stammered Talthybius.

"Yes?" said the mother, anxiously pressing the boy to her. "Surely he goes with me? He is so young!"

"He is little now," said the herald reluctantly, "but his father was a great hero and one whom the Greeks feared. They dare not let the son of such a man grow up to trouble them. The child must die."

"No!" screamed Andromache desperately, tightening her hold upon her son.

"I am charged to say," mumbled Talthybius, "that if you let him go without an outcry, you may bury him with honor and send him down to dwell in Hades happily. If you resist, his corpse will be thrown out unburied in the open plain."

"Let him go," said Hecuba drearily. "They will take him in any case, and we can at least send the son of my great son down to the dead like a prince."

Andromache clasped the child silently, tears streaming down her white face, but she got up when the soldiers came over to her and followed them unresisting. Hecuba sank to the ground again and covered her eyes, listening to the sound of shuffling sandals moving away across the grass.

The Greeks hurled Hector's baby from the highest tower of Troy. After that grim deed Pyrrhus took Andromache

home with him and was as gentle as his nature allowed him
to be, for he loved her dearly. He would not marry her, however, because she was only a slave and he preferred the
daughter of Menelaus and Helen, who had been promised
him before he came to Troy. When this princess saw that
her husband, Pyrrhus, loved his slave girl, her pride was af-
fronted, and she plotted with a cousin to take Pyrrhus' life.

Pyrrhus was slain, but Andromache was saved from her
persecutors and married Helenus, whom the Greeks had
spared because he had told them to capture the Palladium.
Helenus and Andromache never went back to Troy, but they
lived and died in peace, if not in happiness.

Hecuba set out with Odysseus, but she did not live long
after her vengeance on the king of Thrace. Some say that the
gods changed her to a dog whose desolate howling could be
heard ringing through the northern woods. Others declared
that her mind gave way under her troubles, and that she
threw herself overboard to drown.

Troy was razed to the ground, and none of the few who
escaped returned to rebuild it. Antenor and his sons, who
had been granted their lives in return for Theano's treachery
in betraying the Palladium, retired to neighboring cities.
Aeneas and his followers set out for Italy and the long migra-
tions that were to end with the founding of Rome.

PART 6

THE RETURN OF THE HEROES

1

Agamemnon's Death

AS the herald, Talthybius, set out to announce to the daughters of Hecuba their doom, men were already cutting furze for a beacon on the peak of Mount Ida. Presently it flared up and was seen from an island, where watchmen lighted a pile they had been guarding there. Its flames streamed up to heaven, and far down on the horizon the light of the next beacon twinkled in answer to it. On island after island the relayed fires sprang up, and swift as the winds that fanned them, the tidings of Troy's fall flamed across the sea. Soon they raced down the mainland of Greece, until Queen Clytemnestra in her palace at Mycenae knew that the time of reckoning was near.

Ten years had passed, but the queen had never forgotten the murder of Iphigenia, her eldest daughter, whom she had especially loved. Soon after the fleet had sailed, townsmen began to gossip that the queen favored Aegisthus, who was cousin to Agamemnon and his bitter enemy. A few bold spirits threatened openly that when the king came home, his wife would feel his anger. Such men were murdered, imprisoned, or driven into exile. Aegisthus had a guard of armed bullies who terrorized honest people, while a host of paid informers spied out the enemies of the queen. Men learned it was wise to hold their peace and offer silent prayer to the gods for their king's return.

Mycenae was soon buzzing with whispers, as Clytemnestra was seen laying rich presents upon the altars in gratitude for her husband's victory.

"Does the queen really think to deceive Agamemnon?" they wondered. "Does she suppose that the king will not ask for his friends, who have been murdered, or that we will not dare to inform him what was done while he was away?"

Traders, coming inland from small coasting vessels, brought the first news of Agamemnon's approach. "The king's ships were scattered by a storm," they said, "but he is safe and brings much plunder. He has with him the Trojan prophetess, Cassandra, with whom he is strangely in love."

"What will Clytemnestra do now?" wondered the people. "Her pride will never bear this insult."

"None can love my husband as I do," declared Clytemnestra. "All the city knows how I have longed for him when he was away from home."

This statement was received in unfriendly silence, but

Clytemnestra took no notice and went with more offerings to the altars of the gods.

Thus matters stood when the great procession of the conqueror entered Mycenae. Agamemnon rode in a chariot all of gold and was dressed in scarlet. Behind, in a painted chariot drawn by white horses stood pale Cassandra in white robes embroidered with gold and with her hair caught back in a woolen band. Men whispered to one another, but they soon forgot the girl as they gazed at the treasures carried by men-at-arms and slaves. There were the great carved chests of Hecuba and Priam, whence the old man had taken out ransom for the body of Hector, his son. There were drinking cups of solid gold, bronze vessels and armor, chariots inlaid with strange patterns, rich garments, and frightened slaves.

Even more interesting than these to the people of Mycenae was the sight of the battle-worn veterans who followed their master home. Cries of joy were heard, shouts of anxious inquiry, laughter, and bitter tears. Old men cheered for the return of fair rule and justice. Women called out to their husbands or their sons. Children shouted and screamed for joy at the sight of the great procession winding its way through the town toward the palace where Clytemnestra stood on the steps to greet her lord.

Clytemnestra was a tall, gaunt woman whose looks had faded with the passing of years, leaving her nothing but an air of harsh, untamable pride. Her greatest beauty, her glossy hair untouched by gray, was caught in a golden band,

and her long robe of scarlet had deep borders of gold.

King and queen looked at each other, Agamemnon high in
his chariot, his wife on the palace steps. The procession behind the king halted, and the shouting died away. Clytemnestra came slowly down the steps toward her husband and
looked up at him calmly, laying her strong hand on his
chariot rail.

"Welcome, great king and conqueror," said she in loud,
clear tones. "Welcome, my husband, leader of a thousand
ships and the greatest hero on earth! Only my household
can tell how I have longed for you while I tried with my poor
woman's powers to order your kingdom well. Often the task
was so hard that I would have killed myself in despair and
loneliness, had not my servants prevented me. Ask your people!" She turned to the crowd, throwing out her arm in a
magnificent gesture. "With one voice they will tell you how
I have eaten out my heart in your absence and have had no
thought that should not please you on this happy day of your
return."

The townspeople received this outburst in blank silence,
while Agamemnon, who had heard rumors of his wife's conduct as he came down the coast, looked at her doubtfully, unwilling to make reproaches until he had clearer knowledge of
the truth.

"Such conduct as you describe is faithful indeed," he said
after some hesitation, "but now is not the time to talk of it.
We are tired, and have come home to sit at our ease with our
old friends. Later it will be time to speak of how things have

gone with us, when each may be rewarded according to his deserts."

"Bring scarlet cloth!" cried the queen, turning to her servants. "Bring carpets gloriously dyed and precious beyond telling to make a path for the greatest conqueror on earth."

"This is folly," protested Agamemnon, bewildered by the queen's vehemence. "I am no god to walk on scarlet, but a plain man coming home."

"You are a king among kings," insisted she, "and this day you shall not defile your feet."

"Very well," he grumbled ungraciously, anxious to cut short the scene. "I will walk on your carpets, though I call all to witness that I do not care for such pomp."

"Servants!" she cried. "Make ready a bath for the king, who is weary with travel. Bring out the embroidered garments we have made for his return."

Agamemnon leaped down from his chariot, and went in angrily over the shining carpets, his triumph spoiled by the foolish exaggeration of his wife. Clytemnestra followed him, still calling orders to her slaves.

The townsfolk scattered eagerly to greet the returning soldiers, while a great crowd went to watch the treasures being carried in to Agamemnon's storehouse. Only a few people remained in the hot, bright square to gaze curiously at the painted chariot in which Cassandra stood alone. The soldiers had not dared herd her in with the other slaves, while Agamemnon in his haste and embarrassment had forgotten her utterly. Clytemnestra, as she followed her husband, had rudely ordered her rival to enter, but the girl stood looking up at the empty sky and paid no heed.

"Apollo!" called she in low tones, neither seeing nor hearing the curious group that pressed around to see the mad prophetess with whom their king was said to be in love.

"Apollo!" cried Cassandra more loudly. "What house of death is this that smells with the blood of children cruelly slain?"

There was a stir among the people, for long ago, though none cared to speak of it, Agamemnon's father had put his brother's children dreadfully to death.

Cassandra screamed suddenly and pointed at the house roof, her eyes wide with terror. "See how the cow gores the bull and the wife smites her husband. Alas for the net and the bloodstained axe that wait within!"

"What do you mean?" cried a man in the crowd with sudden anxiety.

"Apollo!" cried Cassandra once more, lifting her face to the blazing sun. "I will not die as your servant. Take back your cursed gift that has made me a madwoman and a thing of scorn. If there was happiness in store for any man, I never foresaw it, but my visions have always been terrible down to this last moment of all. I must go in out of the sunlight to my death, but first I will tear from my head the white band marking me your priestess, and die free."

She threw the band down and trod deliberately upon it. Stepping out of the chariot, she walked slowly up the steps toward the door. There she paused a moment, conscious perhaps for the first time of the crowd behind her. "It is a dreadful thing for the lord of a thousand ships," she said distinctly, "to be cast out unburied in the rain." Before any man could trouble her with questions, she was gone into the shadow of the dark door.

Agamemnon entered his house sulkily with his wife behind him. The slaves were not good enough to do him service, she proclaimed. She herself, the queen, would attend him to his bath. She took his sword as he unbuckled it, exclaiming reverently over the deeds it had wrought. "Let me hang it on this peg across the room," said she, "lest the damp steam tarnish its splendor, for it is the sword of a great king."

The king stepped into the warm water and lay back in the bath at his ease.

"Let me gather up your garments, for you must wear fresh ones at the feast," she said, coming round the head of the bath and stooping, as if to pick up the clothes. Suddenly she rose behind her husband with a great net in her arms that she had laid ready, and with a quick movement enveloped him from head to foot.

Agamemnon exclaimed in surprise and tried to scramble up, but he was wet and his arms were entangled. Before he could get free, the queen had snatched up an axe and turned on him. Heaving up her weapon with both hands, she clenched her teeth and hewed her husband down with all her strength.

The blow fell between neck and shoulder and bit deep. The king gave a great cry as he slipped in the water, which had suddenly turned a dreadful red. He got one hand on the edge of the bath and pulled himself up, calling desperately for help. Frantic with hate and terror, the woman struck again and again.

"You would drive me out for that madwoman's sake?" she panted. "You murderer of my daughter!"

The king lay still at last. Clytemnestra lifted her dripping axe and strode through the doorway. In the hall, the frightened servants recoiled at her approach.

"Where is the woman?" she demanded menacingly. "Where is that Trojan slave for whom my husband would have forsaken me?"

All eyes turned on the doorway, against which leaned the small figure of the shrinking girl. Clytemnestra came across the floor, and Cassandra with an effort stood up straight, waiting proudly for her doom.

2

The Adventures
of Menelaus

KING Menelaus came sword in hand in search of Helen, his prize after ten year's war. He found her amid the captive women, like a sun among pale stars. Helen's hair was as golden as ever, and her clear skin unlined by age. Indeed, she seemed even more lovely than his dim memories of her, so that for all his anger, he could not destroy her while she smiled at him.

"Kill her!" urged Hecuba fiercely. "Such a woman is not fit to live!"

Menelaus wavered. "Let me at least hear what she has to say."

"Husband," said Helen, turning to him with a gesture of infinite grace, "you must not blame me for the schemes of Aphrodite. Is it my fault that the goddess chose me out of

205

all women to be the bride of her favorite, Paris? Could I resist her enchantment? When Paris died and the spell was broken, you cannot know how I longed to come home. Odysseus will tell you that I aided him then and sent him safe out of Troy, but none will describe how often I tried to escape and was restrained."

"That is all a lie," cried Hecuba desperately. "Kill her before she wheedles forgiveness out of you."

Menelaus bit his lip and frowned in an effort to recover his anger, and he looked helplessly down at the drawn sword in his hand. With sudden decision he put it back in its sheath. "I will take her home to Sparta for judgment," said he sharply, turning away. "She shall sail in a separate ship, for I will not listen to her prayers."

Such was the decision of Menelaus, but he was not destined to reach home as rapidly as he had planned. The gods, who had abandoned Troy to the Greeks, were now outraged by the violation of their temples and the plundering of their images. In revenge they raised a great storm to scatter the ships of the returning fleet. Menelaus, driven eastward far out of his course, came with the loss of many ships to Egypt, where he remained some years before the ruler of that land would permit him to return home. In such circumstances he was thrown together with Helen, so that after a while she won him again.

Some writers declare that Menelaus discovered Helen living in Egypt and found that she had never actually been at Troy at all. The gods, they say, wishing to bring about Troy's destruction, had made an image of Helen, which Paris was permitted to carry away. The true Helen, meanwhile, was

transported to Egypt, where she longed in vain for her husband until he discovered her there on his way home. When
the false Helen vanished into air, Menelaus was reunited
to his faithful wife.

However this may be, all agree that Menelaus was reconciled with his wife in Egypt, where he was long delayed. Even
when he set out at last, he lay for a great while hopelessly becalmed on a little island off the mouth of the Nile.

Here the Spartans almost perished of starvation, for the
island was barren; but at last Menelaus was helped by a
sea nymph who met him wandering hopelessly along the
shore.

"Ask the advice of the sea god, Proteus, the wise one of the
deep," was her counsel. "He will know how to aid you if you
can but force him to speak."

"How shall a man force a god?" asked the hero in despair.

"If you can catch him and hold him when he comes up the
beach with his flock of seals to sleep in the sun, he will tell
you whatever you ask. Come here at daybreak tomorrow, and
I will show you how to lay hands on the god."

Early the next morning while the sky was still gray with the
approach of dawn, Menelaus and three chosen companions
came down to the beach. The goddess gave each one the skin
of a seal, bidding him scoop a hollow in the sand and cover
himself over. For a long time they waited anxiously, half
smothered by the smell of fish and seaweed as the hot sun
arose and beat on the damp skins.

When midmorning came, the seals of Proteus' flock began
to wallow out of the breakers and edge themselves, groaning,
up the beach. They settled themselves in a huddled group,

almost touching the four skins that lay drying there. After much thumping and blowing, there was finally silence, except for a loud, harsh, snoring sound.

The stench of the warm sea creatures was intolerable now, and Menelaus cautiously lifted a corner of the skin. A slow, humped wave was traveling in to the land. He watched it break on the beach with a sullen roar, while out of it, puffing heavily, wallowed a strange old man. Seaweed dripped from his beard and hung from the ends of his garments as he came lurching up the beach, groaning over the little ridges of sand. He stood over the seals to count his flock, starting with the four at the end whose skins the goddess had stolen. Presently he nodded to himself and sat down heavily in a pool formed by the water dripping from him, in the midst of which he steamed in the sun.

Menelaus threw off the sealskin and seized him, shouting to the others. The god opened his eyes with a start, twitched, and changed in a flash to a snarling lion. Menelaus and his comrades clutched it by the mane, nothing dismayed, when it suddenly turned to a smooth snake, gliding out of their hands. Hastily they tightened their grip, but now the god was a leopard, and then a huge boar whose struggles dragged his captors helpless over the ground. Still they held tight until the god changed to water, which ran through their fingers. Menelaus hurled himself bodily on top of a little pool soaking into the ground. Even as he gathered up some in his palms, he felt himself lifted into air and found himself hanging by one hand from a branch of a tall flowering tree. The branch broke, but Menelaus caught at another and

heaved himself across it, panting. At that the god gave up the struggle and turned back to his own shape.

"Some one of the immortals must have instructed you, Spartan King," he said, "and with them it is useless to struggle. Ask me what you wish, but quickly, for I long for the cool water."

"How shall I get home to Sparta?" demanded Menelaus eagerly. "I have been long in Egypt, and before that I was ten years at Troy. Now I am becalmed on this island while my men starve. Is there to be no end to my wanderings?"

"Return to Egypt," said the god, "and make offerings for a fair wind. It is hard to go back over the misty deep when you have come so far toward home, but if you do not, you will never see Sparta or Mycenae."

"I must go then," said Menelaus sighing, "though the way will be weary. Am I the last to come home from Troy and the only one who is not reigning happily in his kingdom, rejoicing in his immortal fame?"

"Three men were not so fortunate. One is living and two are dead."

"Who are these?" inquired Menelaus eagerly. "It is long since I had news of the kings who fought at Troy."

"Do not seek to know their names. You will learn them soon enough."

Menelaus tightened his grip on the god. "Tell me their stories," said he.

Proteus moved restlessly in the sun and sighed. "Ajax Oileus was the first to die. It was Ajax who plundered the temple of Athene in Troy; wherefore the goddess prevailed on Poseidon to raise a great storm, which scattered the fleet."

"I should well remember that storm," nodded Menelaus. "Many brave men were drowned; Ajax Oileus, I suppose, among the number."

"He was drowned, though not straightway, for when his ship went down, he leaped into the sea clutching a piece of wreckage. Half drifting and half swimming he came in to shore, where a great wave lifted him and dashed him against the rocks. Bruised though he was, however, he managed to find a crack and to twist his fingers in it, so that when the wave receded, it did not carry him out to sea. As the next wave raised him up, he scrambled for a hold with his feet. Thus though bleeding and battered, he gained the top of the rock, where he was clear of the thundering waters.

"It seemed as though he were saved, and so he would have been had he not lifted up his voice and screamed defiance at the winds and waters. 'I have saved myself by my own efforts,' cried he, 'and I will live in the gods' despite.'

"At that Poseidon smote the sea with his trident, and a wave huge as a mountain fell with a thunderous crash on the rock. With a mighty rumble the whole cliff split apart, and Ajax, still clutching it vainly, fell into the boiling foam and disappeared."

"I am sorry to hear he is dead," said Menelaus, "for he was a brave man and a wonderful runner. No man ever beat him but Achilles, except once when his foot slipped. Tell me now, who else of the heroes is dead?"

"Your brother, Agamemnon," said the god reluctantly. "His own wife, Clytemnestra, murdered him on his triumph day and now rules over Mycenae with Aegisthus, your enemy, as her lord. Vengeance is near her, however, from her son,

Orestes, who bestirs himself to kill her for his father's sake."

"My brother, my brother!" said Menelaus, letting go the god and covering his eyes with his hand. "To think that the leader of a thousand ships should come to so pitiful an end!"

"One wanderer is yet more unhappy," said the god, looking at him with compassion. "Odysseus' ships are all lost, and he himself is imprisoned on a far-off island by Calypso, a sea nymph. All day long he sits on the beach looking out over the gray ocean in the direction of his home. Great tears of longing roll down his cheeks, but in vain, for years are yet to pass before he sets foot in Ithaca once more."

The god turned and waddled down over the sand toward the water at a surprising speed. As a wave reared its head to meet him, he stepped into it and was gone. Menelaus turned to his friends.

"Come," said he. "Bid the men drag our ships down to the water and place the masts and sails within. Let us make ready to start back to Egypt, for it is a long and weary way."

Menelaus set forth and delayed long enough in Egypt for the sacrifices and prayers the jealous gods demanded of him. Eventually he came back to Sparta, where he lived peacefully for a long time, and all things were as before. Every evening Helen would come into his hall and sit spinning bright-colored wool from her fair, silver basket. If the old minstrel's songs grew tedious, she made no sign, for she was gentler to her husband than of old. She still loved to talk of far lands with traveling strangers, but when she saw Menelaus watched her jealously, she would arise with her marvelous grace and depart for her chamber. Her adventures were over, and she chiefly wished to live out her life in peace.

3

Nestor at Home

OLD Nestor in his kingdom of Pylos was for the ninth time since his return performing the yearly sacrifices offered to Poseidon, lord of the sea. For this his strength still sufficed, but after the ceremonies were over, he was glad to sit down in the shade of a rock on soft sheepskins his servants had strewed for him. Here he leaned back to wait while the feast was prepared and closed his eyes, scarcely hearing the chatter of his companions and sons about a ship rounding the headland and rowing in toward the shore.

The ship ran out of sight up the mouth of a little river, but presently an old man and a youth approached over the dunes from the direction of its landing place. The elder, though he carried a staff, went ahead with swift strides and erect, confident bearing. The young man who followed was simply dressed in a plain white tunic, but he moved with a marvelous grace, and his sword was studded with silver like the weapon of a prince.

Pisistratus, Nestor's youngest son, jumped up and ran to greet the strangers. He smiled at the youth and clasped his hand as he bade the pair welcome, for Nestor liked old men about him, and his young son felt often alone. Courtesy now forbade him to ask the guests their business, but he made a place for them on the soft rugs by his father and brought meat and wine, first to the old man and then to the young.

Nestor, who set great store by all the old forms of politeness, addressed no questions to the strangers while they satisfied their hunger and thirst. Not until their meal was over did he put his own meat aside and ask them their names. "Are you traders perhaps," he inquired, "or adventurers out to gain plunder and glory across the sea?"

The elder man answered never a word, though Nestor's question had been addressed chiefly to him. Instead he turned to his companion, smiling, and the youth, seeing himself appealed to, blushed fiery red. In a moment, however, he mastered himself and answered courteously, "We come from a little island, O King, good only for the pasturing of goats and the culture of bees. Nevertheless you have heard its name, for it is Ithaca, and its king was Odysseus, my father, who was judged the greatest of heroes after Achilles' death."

"You must be Telemachus, then," said old Nestor, smiling. "It does my heart good to hear your voice, which reminds me of your father's. Ah, Odysseus was a man of extraordinary wisdom! In all the years we two were at Troy, our counsel always agreed!" He paused for a moment, collecting his thoughts, and would have said more, since harmless vanity was his chief weakness and he loved to talk of himself. Telemachus, however, leaned earnestly forward like a man who cannot wait to unburden his mind.

"Can you give me news of my father?" said he eagerly. "Not a ship or man who sailed for Troy with Odysseus has ever come home. No tidings either good or bad have reached us at all."

"It is almost ten years since Troy was taken," said Nestor, shaking his head solemnly. "If he had not returned by now, he is surely dead."

"It would have been better far for my mother and myself if he had been," Telemachus answered gloomily. "All the unruly nobles of the land have for a long time aspired to marry my mother and enjoy her possessions. Had she chosen one of them, the land would have had a tyrant, perhaps, but as it is, we have many. My mother's suitors have taken possession of our house, where they live in lawlessness and riot. Old Mentor, here, tells me that now I am a man and have taken it upon me to inquire for my father, they are even plotting against my life."

"Alas," said Nestor sadly. "Tidings come rarely from Ithaca, which lies far away in the western sea. How can such men think to force your mother to marry against her will?"

"She cannot help herself. At first she pretended that she could not wed until she had finished a shroud for my grandfather, Laertes. For a while, therefore, the suitors left her alone, while she set up a loom in her chamber and started an intricate pattern such as might take a woman a year. For many hours she worked at it daily, but at night when all were asleep, she would steal out and rip up what she had woven, so that the work progressed little, if at all. It was long before the wooers suspected, but they caught her at last and are forcing her to finish the shroud and to choose a new husband. My father, if he is still living, must come back, or it will be too late."

"I will tell you what I know of the return of the Greeks," answered Nestor, "though I have little to say of Odysseus. King Agamemnon wished the host to remain some days after the taking of Troy in order to appease by sacrifices the anger of the gods whose temples had been plundered. Most of us, however, were frantic for home and thought it better to outrun the storm the Olympians threatened to raise against us. Pyrrhus left first, since ill news had come to him of war in the kingdom of his grandfather, Peleus. After him I fled, and Odysseus came with me, thinking that we would force Agamemnon to follow if we all put to sea. When, however, Agamemnon still stayed for the sacrifices, Odysseus parted from me and returned to the shore. That is all I know of his fortunes."

Mentor raised his head and broke silence. "Agamemnon came safely home in spite of the anger of the gods," he observed.

"Better would it have been for Agamemnon if the storm he met at sea had swallowed him up. By preserving him and sending him home, the gods took more terrible revenge."

"Odysseus, then, must have met the storm also," said Telemachus thoughtfully. "Is it possible that he and all his men were drowned?"

"It is not likely, for though the ships were all scattered, the sea swallowed none of the heroes but Ajax Oileus, who had angered Athene. Most of those who perished were lured onto the rocks by Palamedes' father, Nauplius, who lit beacon lights to deceive the ships seeking shelter from the storm. Nauplius did this in vengeance for his son's death, which we all know came about through the agency of Odysseus. If, therefore, Ithacans had been wrecked along those coasts, Nauplius would surely have boasted openly that his enemy was dead."

"Who else was caught in this storm?"

"Fair-haired Menelaus was driven over the waters to Egypt and did not reach his home, they say, for seven years. He has wandered far and may have news of your father which no other hero is likely to have gained. Philoctetes sailed ahead of us with Pyrrhus. Diomede was close behind me and also escaped the storm. Even Teucer reached Salamis safely, though his father drove him away again with bitter reproaches because he had dared to come alive while Ajax, his brother, was dead."

"It is best, then, that I go to Menelaus," declared Telemachus, musing. "Before I make this journey, however, you must tell me how things stand in Mycenae and Sparta. Has Menelaus avenged the murder of his brother, and is he master in his own land?"

"Clytemnestra!" said old Nestor thoughtfully, shaking his white head over her name. "She would never have ruled in Mycenae if Menelaus had come home. As it was, she was slain in the seventh year by Orestes, her own son and Agamemnon's, who they say was driven out of his mind by the horror of his deed. Menelaus dwells at peace with Helen in Sparta. I wonder if she is as beautiful now!"

Telemachus smiled unbelievingly. "My father wooed her once," he remarked, "but that was over twenty years ago."

Mentor stirred a little and drew his cloak about him. "The sun is going down," said he. "Let us pour our last cup of wine on the sand in Poseidon's honor before Telemachus and I return to our ship."

"May the gods forbid that you should sleep on shipboard as though you had come to visit a man who had neither beds nor blankets," cried Nestor hastily. "Never while I or my children live shall a son of Odysseus be turned away from my house. Tomorrow I will give you a chariot and horses, while Pisistratus will gladly guide you to the palace of Menelaus, which lies inland."

"I am too old for the jolting of a chariot," agreed Mentor. "Let Pisistratus go with you, while I return to the ship and reassure the seamen. Do not be surprised if I am gone before you return, for I have set you on the road to find your father, and I have other tasks to do."

He rose, and the setting sun fell full on his white head, turning it to a glory of silver. The heroes blinked at it, dazzled, and when they opened their eyes again, Mentor was gone. In the distance a great black eagle went sailing down the wind.

"Some god has brought you on this journey," said Nestor to Telemachus in awe. "Take courage, for now I know that you will find your father, since the immortals themselves are guiding you."

4

In the House of the Swineherd

EUMAEUS, the king's swineherd, was sitting in the doorway of his house, busily cutting new sandals for himself out of a good, tough piece of oxhide, rejoicing in the solitude and quiet of noon. Three of his herdsmen had driven out the swine to root for acorns under the oaks of Corax, while the fourth had gone into the city with a fat pig for Penelope's wooers, who demanded supplies from the herds of Odysseus every day.

With a sudden howl one of the dogs raced over the yard to the gateway, followed by the rest of the snarling pack. Eumaeus threw aside his work and jumped up in time to see them fall on a white-haired beggar who was coming slowly up to the gate.

The stranger seemed used to dogs. Instead of resisting, he

dropped his staff and sat down placidly on a small rock by the side of the path. The dogs hesitated for a moment, puzzled, and before they had made up their minds to attack, Eumaeus scattered them yelping with a shower of stones.

"Come in, old man," he called out, panting. "My dogs are trained to be savage with strangers, so that it is well that you did not strike them, or you might easily have lost your life. Tell me how you come to be wandering on this little island where every man is known to me by sight."

The beggar followed his host into the hut and sat down on a thick goatskin rug the swineherd spread for him. "I was always a wanderer," said he in a deep, musical voice, at the sound of which the swineherd started and looked at him curiously. "I was at the seige of Troy, but when others went home, I alone met further adventure. I have passed by enchanted islands set in strange, blue seas, where men have been bewitched of their memories or changed into groveling swine. I have crossed the great whirlpool, Charybdis, which sucks whole ships into its gulf, and journeyed as far as the lands of perpetual twilight that lie at the ends of the earth. I have even dined on a brazen island with Aeolus, king of the winds, who imprisoned all but the breeze that blew homeward and gave them me tied in a sack. My last adventure has cast me up on your island, through which I am wandering to the city to beg my bread."

"Surely if you have traveled so far, you have heard of our lost king, Odysseus," inquired the swineherd eagerly. "I know well enough that his bones were washed clean long ago on the floor of the ocean and are now silted over with sand.

Odysseus is certainly dead, and it would be far better for Penelope to know this than to let the land fall into hopeless confusion while she waits for our lord to come home."

"Odysseus is not dead," said the old man with certainty. "A short while ago I was guest in a country through which he had lately passed on his long, homeward voyage. I may have reached Ithaca ahead of him, but before the old moon wanes once more, he will surely return to take vengeance on those who have dishonored his house."

"How like that is to a beggar!" retorted Eumaeus scornfully. "Well you know that Queen Penelope will richly reward a man who brings her such a tale! Odysseus is dead, I am sure, and you had best keep your story to yourself, lest you fall foul of Penelope's suitors, who show little respect for gray hairs."

The beggar shrugged lightly. "Well, I think I will go to the city," he declared. "I am too old to work for my bread, and you cannot supply me with clothing, though as you see this garment will very soon fall off my back."

Eumaeus shrugged in his turn, and changing the subject began to complain of the suitors and of how the flocks and herds of Odysseus had dwindled to half their size. "With my own hands I have fenced in this courtyard and built my house and these sties," he declared. "I have even bought my own servants to help me, since Penelope cannot oversee these affairs. My master would have seen to such matters himself and not have left me to struggle unaided. Small wonder that men like Melanthius, the goatherd, make their fortunes by serving the wooers in the palace and neglecting their herds."

Eumaeus was still reciting the endless roll of his troubles when they both heard the noise of the swineherds driving in the sows for the night. Eumaeus went out to pen them all in and to order the men to prepare meat for the evening meal. It was still early when dinner was over and they began to strew beds of fresh branches close to the fire. "Lie here," said Eumaeus to the old man. "I sleep outside near my herd."

"Odysseus is lucky indeed to have such a servant!" remarked the old beggar as he curled himself up in a cloak and turned away his face from the flame.

Next morning the herdsmen, who rose with the dawn, were out with the swine before the beggar and Eumaeus had leisure for preparing their breakfast. Eumaeus, as though night had not intervened, was pouring out a steady stream of his troubles, this time concerning Telemachus, whom he evidently loved. " . . . and so he took the ship and made off in secret to look for his father," he was saying, "and the wooers have sent out a ship to ambush him on his return, so that we all fear for his life."

"Someone is coming," the beggar interrupted him. "The dogs have run out to meet him, but they are not barking, so that I would judge they know him well."

Eumaeus, who had a great bowl in his hands full of wine and water which he had been mixing, looked up to behold a bright-haired young man just entering the courtyard gate. "It is Telemachus, my master!" cried he, dropping the bowl with a crash on the floor and running out through the doorway, where he fell to kissing the young man's hands and stroking his hair.

"Give thanks to the gods who preserved me," said Telemachus eagerly. "It was they who warned me of the ambush as I came hastening home after hearing from King Menelaus that my father is certainly alive. A god bade me land on this side of the island and come to your hut instead of to the city, where the wooers might still threaten my life."

"That is very well," replied Eumaeus, "for it happens by chance that I have an old man in my hut, a poor beggar, who may take any message to Penelope without being suspected."

"It is better that Eumaeus go himself," said the old man, appearing in the doorway, "for Penelope knows him. Moreover, he can warn your best friends among the townspeople to protect you, so that tomorrow you may go openly home."

"You are a wise man, I see," cried the swineherd, "and your counsel is good. Come in, my dear master, and sit here while I put on my sandals and run for the city. If I go now, I shall be back here by evening with news."

He went chattering out into the courtyard with the old beggarman at his heels. Presently the beggar returned alone and stood silent in the doorway, filling it from side to side with the breadth of his shoulders. Telemachus cast a careless glance at him and gave a sudden start of astonishment.

"Forgive me," he said slowly, rising to his feet, "for my eyes have once more deceived me. I thought you were a dirty old beggar, and behold, you are a god. A moment ago you were twisted and scarred and your beard was ragged with age. Now you are more majestic than mortals are, a king in the prime of life. Gods love such changes in form."

"This is my own shape," said the stranger quietly. "The

other was a disguise put upon me by the goddess Athene. Do you not know who I am?"

Telemachus shook his head wordlessly as he watched the tears gather in the great, gray eyes of the stranger. "I am your father, Odysseus," said the latter in a choking voice, "at home, in Ithaca, after twenty years."

He stretched out his arms to his son, and Telemachus fell on his breast and embraced him. There was a long silence in the dark hut, for the hearts of both were far too full for speech. At last, however, Odysseus led his son to a seat by the wall where the swineherd had laid thick goatskins over a rude settle of wood.

"Sit down, my son," said he, "and leave all your questions for later. You and I must plan the death of the suitors who have brought so much evil on our house."

5

The Bow Is Bent

QUEEN Penelope flung wide the door of her treasure chamber, where lay her coffers of beautiful garments, together with the trophies of bronze, gold, or iron that Odysseus had won. Tears came into her eyes as she reached for a bow enclosed in a bright case of leather that hung from a peg on the wall. She sat down on a chest for a while with the bow on her knees as she thought of her famous husband and of her twenty lonely years. It was time, she knew, to make an end of her troubles, so she drew the bow from its case with a steady hand, took the quiver, and called to her maidens to attend her to the great hall.

This afternoon the wooers sat at their tables, each with a winecup before him, which the goatherd, Melanthius, was keeping filled. They were in an evil humor because Telemachus had returned safely and seemed to have grown in

manhood from his voyage abroad. For instance, an old beggar had wandered into the hall, but when they had wished to
make him the butt of their jokes, Telemachus had intervened. They had let the old man alone in the end, not so
much because Telemachus bade them as because he himself
was a sturdy rascal and had given a man who interfered with
him such a buffet that the fellow had been dragged out half
dead. They contented themselves with a few loud jokes about
the sort of guest Telemachus favored, but little groups in the
corners of the hall were discussing means of murdering the
young prince who was learning to defy them.

All looked up in surprise as Penelope herself appeared in
the door. Each man began to call out for the queen to sit by
him, though she seldom came in while they were feasting and
had hitherto showed favor to none.

Penelope's hair was still dark and as thick as Odysseus remembered it. Her face was pale, however, and her figure was
heavier, though it had gained in dignity through the years.
As the tumult died somewhat, she spoke in the deep, clear
tones that he remembered so well.

"The web I was weaving is finished at last, and the hope
that I long cherished has died away. Hear me, then, O my
suitors, since it seems to me better to choose one lord from
among you than to suffer these outrages daily at the hands
of you all. I will marry the man who can string the bow of
Odysseus and shoot one of his arrows through the holes of
twelve axes set in a row. Odysseus himself could perform
this feat, and I do not care to wed with a lesser man."

She gave the bow to the swineherd, who had come into the

hall early that morning, and who by chance stood nearest the door. He and Telemachus together set up the axes, and then stood aside while the first of the wooers got up to try the bow. Leiodes was the man's name, a soothsayer, a good man at heart, yet dragged along by the others. Now he strove till he bruised his unworn, delicate hands, which had never known labor; yet for all his efforts, he could not manage the bow.

"I cannot bend it," he admitted at last. "Hard though it is to fail of such a prize, I must be content like many another. I do not think we shall easily master such a weapon."

"You are a fool," retorted Antinous, the handsomest and haughtiest of the wooers. "Must we all fail to bend the bow just because you have no strength in your hands? Blow up the fire, Melanthius, and bring out some lard. We will warm the bow and grease it thoroughly before we test our strength."

Melanthius did as he was told, and the young men rubbed the bow and held it to the fire, but in vain. Even Eurymachus, the leader among them, could not bend it at all.

"Let it alone for tonight," said Antinous at last. "Tomorrow we will sacrifice to the gods and pray to them for strength before we try again."

All agreed with relief and sat down again at their tables, while the serving maids hastened to bring water for washing and to pour it over their hands. The suitors began to drink and laugh among themselves, until over the hubbub Antinous heard the voice of the beggar actually asking to handle the bow.

"It is not that I want a rich wife at my age," he was saying. "A new cloak and tunic will surely be plenty for me. Still, I used to be skillful with the bow when I was much younger, and I am curious to know whether my strength has deserted me yet."

"Insolent rascal!" shouted Antinous. "Hold your tongue, and leave such weapons to princes, to whom they belong."

"The bow is mine," said Penelope clearly from her seat beside the door, "and I say that the beggar shall handle it if he will, though he may not win me for a bride."

"No, mother," said Telemachus calmly. "The bow was my father's once, but now it is mine. Go to your room for tonight, since the trial is over, and leave me to lend my belongings to what man I will."

Penelope, who had never before heard her son speak as master of the house, was lost in amazement. She rose without a word and mounted the steep stairs to her chamber, where she wept for her long-lost husband until Athene sent sleep on her eyes.

Meanwhile, in the great hall Eumaeus brought the bow over to the beggar, who took it in his hands, inspecting every inch with a careful eye.

"So you stand with Telemachus, swineherd?" called one of the men. "You will live to regret obeying his orders when the day comes for a better man to rule."

Those who sat in the corners laughed grimly, their eyes on Telemachus. Of a sudden the old beggar, putting forth his strength, bent the bow quickly and easily, slipping the string into its notch. Catching up an arrow from beside him, without even rising from his seat, he sent it clear through the holes in the axes and into the wall.

One or two of the wooers started up with a cry, but the beggar man flung aside his tattered cloak and leaped for the threshold. "Now for a better mark," thundered he as he sent a keen arrow straight through the throat of Antinous, who with head back was in the act of draining a two-handled cup of wine.

Antinous fell with a crash, dropping his cup and overturning the table before him with his feet. The wooers jumped up, and many turned instinctively to the walls where the weapons of Odysseus' household were usually hung. All the pegs were empty, however, since Telemachus had taken the armor away that morning under the pretext that it was being spoiled by the smoke and must all be cleaned.

"Dogs!" thundered the beggar from the doorway. "You thought that I should never come home from the land of the Trojans, and that you might safely lay waste my house and force yourselves on my wife against her will. Now I am here, and the day of payment is come."

A great hush fell on the wooers as they looked on one another in dismay, none knowing what answer to make. After a pause Eurymachus said, "If you are indeed Odysseus of Ithaca, it is true that you have been wronged, but this was the fault of Antinous, who urged us all on. Now that he is dead, we will pay you for what we have wasted, and more if you please."

Odysseus looked at him, frowning terribly and with the

great bow ready in his hands. "Eurymachus," said he with menace, "not all you have and all you hope to gain would buy your life from me."

"At him with your swords," cried Eurymachus desperately. "Hold up the tables as shields and rush him before he slays us all."

Even as he put a hand to his weapon, an arrow stretched him groaning, while the others started forward in fury or cowered under tables in vain search of escape.

Meanwhile the swineherd and another faithful old servant hastened to close the gate of the courtyard, lest help be brought to the suitors from the town. Telemachus raced for the armory, knowing well that his father's arrows would soon be spent. "Take shield and spear," called he to the two servants, "and stand by my father, lest the suitors rush him while he arms himself."

The suitors now collected their forces and fell on the four men in the doorway, seeking to overwhelm them by numbers while Odysseus was putting on his armor. One man, who sprang forward boldly, fell with a crash, transfixed between the shoulders by Telemachus' spear. Those nearest gave ground again, while Telemachus, not waiting to pull out the weapon, seized another he had placed behind him against the wall.

"We cannot fight unarmored in this fashion," cried Melanthius to those who stood near him. "Help me climb up to the windows, and I can scramble along the roof that runs below them until I reach the armory where the weapons are stored.

Only keep them all busy by the doorway, lest they send someone up to catch me there ''

One of the suitors pushed a table against the wall and
leaped upon it, while two more hoisted the goatherd onto his
shoulders. Melanthius scrambled through the window and
disappeared. Two men stood waiting for his return, but
the others were not eager to rush upon certain death and
stood in a ring around Odysseus until Melanthius should
bring them shields and spears. He thrust what he had
through the window into the arms of those beneath and raced
back for more. Meanwhile, however, Odysseus had seen what
was going on.

"Someone is bringing weapons from the armory," he said
sharply. "Let the two herdsmen go up to bolt the doors.
Telemachus and I may keep the doorway, since these men
are waiting for more weapons before they fall on us."

Melanthius was still in the armory when the herdsmen
reached it. Telemachus had hidden most of the armor, and
Melanthius had so far only discovered one more helmet and
an old, rusty shield that Laertes, Odysseus' father, had borne
when he was young. As Melanthius came past the doorway
with these things in his hand, the two men jumped upon him,
bore him struggling to the floor, and bound him fast.

"The armory is bolted now," said the swineherd briefly as
he returned to take his stand before the door.

"That is good," answered Odysseus. "Your return is
timely, since these dogs, in despair of receiving more armor,
are lining up their spearsmen to attack. Let them throw first,

and avoid their weapons. Afterward hurl with all your strength, for the crowd of them is so great that you can hardly fail to hit some mark."

Six spearsmen ran up the hall toward the doorway with swordsmen pressing behind to rush their enemies when the spears should have wounded them. In the confusion and haste, however, all six threw wide, while the four champions in the doorway, aiming at the mass before them, each slew a man.

The wooers fell back in confusion, dragging with them the bodies of the dead for the sake of the weapons in them. Once more they charged up the hall, and again four of them fell.

The ranks now dissolved in wild confusion, each man seizing a spear as one came to hand and hurling it over the heads of his own friends as best he might. Telemachus and Eumaeus were bleeding slightly, but they still fought like wolves, and Odysseus between them was a raging lion. Leaping out from the threshold, he fell into the midst of his enemies, hacking, thrusting, slashing with such furious force that no man within reach of him was safe. The wooers scattered at last and fled screaming before him, while he pursued them raging, his red sword dripping blood.

"Spare me!" cried Leiodes, the soothsayer, falling on his knees. "I have never insulted Penelope or spread ruin in your halls, but have often asked the others to restrain themselves. Do not kill the innocent with the guilty in your wrath."

"If you were innocent," said Odysseus sternly, "why did

you not go home? You have shared the feasts of the wooers and trial of the bow. Now share their death also."

The wretched man put out his hands and cowered away from the blow, but in vain. The sword met him where the neck joins the shoulder, stretching him in the dust.

Phemius, the minstrel, put down his lyre by the high seat inlaid with silver where Odysseus had been used to sit. "Have pity on me," he implored coming forward trembling. "I am no suitor of Penelope, but have been forced to sing at the feasts of the wooers sorely against my will."

"He speaks truth," said Telemachus quickly. "Spare him, and spare the servant, Medon, who had charge of me when I was a child."

"Where is Medon?"

"Here!" cried the servant eagerly, scrambling out from under the high seat where he had been hiding with a skin wrapped around him for better protection. "Here I am! I have done nothing! Let me alone!"

Odysseus laughed and turned around to view his hall all spattered with meat and wine, and strewn with wrecked tables and the bodies of the dead. "Telemachus," said he, "call servants to help us carry these bodies out and clean the hall."

It was very late that night when the old nurse of the household went up into Penelope's chamber and touched her shoulder, saying in a breathless voice between tears and laughter, "Wake up, dear child. Odysseus is come! Your husband is here, and the suitors who troubled you are slain."

Penelope turned her head a little and looked at the nurse, unbelieving. "What an idle tale!" she said sleepily. "Do not be foolish, nurse."

"It is true," insisted the nurse. "Do you think I could dream the death of your wooers? Come down and see. Odysseus is altered, but I knew him by the scar of a wound on his leg that a boar gave him long ago."

"It is some god," said the queen rising hastily. "Odysseus himself was long ago lost in the ocean and will never return."

Penelope came slowly into the hall and looked at Odysseus, who sat by a pillar in the light of the fire. Her heart leaped within her for a moment at the sight of his broad shoulders, but as she looked on his face, she thought, "It is not he!"

She sat down over against him without a word, noting the curly hair and the deep, gray eyes. "He is very like Odysseus," she said to herself, "yet this is not my husband, but some god. Such majesty and wisdom belong only to one who has seen all things on the wide earth."

"Strange lady!" said the man by the fire in deep tones that she remembered well. "Have you no word of welcome for the husband for whom you have waited so long?"

"It cannot be he!" thought Penelope, twisting her hands in her lap.

"Nurse!" she called out loud. "My husband is home and is weary. Bring out the marriage bed from our chamber and lay blankets and skins thereon."

"How can that be?" asked Odysseus, smiling. "When I built our bridal chamber and the marriage bed that lies within, I took the stem of a living tree still rooted in earth and made it a bedpost. This was a secret sign of our steadfast love, and none knew it but you and I."

Penelope ran across the floor to Odysseus and took his head in her arms, weeping for joy. "Forgive me that I did not know you," said she, "but I have always feared lest some imposter should pass himself off upon me in your place. I spoke of the bed to prove you because by myself I dared not be sure. Men change in twenty years!"

Odysseus put his arms about her and held her. The two wept quietly together over the long years of suffering behind them, but their hearts were singing for joy at the thought of new life ahead.

A LIST OF
Characters and Places

A-CHIL'-LES	Son of Peleus and Thetis and the greatest Greek hero.
AE-GIS'-THUS	Cousin of Agamemnon and lover of Clytemnestra.
AE-NE'-AS	Son of Aphrodite and Anchises, destined to survive Troy's fall and to found a new nation.
AE'-O-LUS	King of the winds, visited by Odysseus on his travels.
AG-A-MEM'-NON	King of Mycenae and overlord of Greece.
A'-JAX	Son of Oileus. The lesser Ajax, a swift runner.
A'-JAX	Son of Telamon. The most powerful Greek hero after Achilles.
A-LEX-AN'-DROS	Another name for Paris.
AM'-A-ZONS	A nation of women fighters.
AN-CHIS'-ES	Father of Aeneas and cousin of Priam.
AN-DROM'-A-CHE	Wife of Hector.
AN-TEN'-OR	Counselor of Priam and leader of the peace party in Troy.
AN-TIL'-O-CHUS	Eldest son of Nestor.
AN-TIN'-O-US	Handsomest of Penelope's suitors.
AN'-TIPH-OS	A son of Priam, killed by Agamemnon.
APH-RO-DI'-TE	Goddess of beauty and chief supporter of the Trojans.
A-POL'-LO	God of the sun and a supporter of the Trojans.
A'-RES	God of war and a supporter of the Trojans.

AR'-GOS	The kingdom of Diomede.
AR'-TEM-IS	Goddess of the moon and a supporter of the Trojans.
ATH-E'-NE	Goddess of wisdom and chief supporter of the Greeks.
AU'-LIS	Place where the Greek fleet gathered and where Agamemnon sacrificed his daughter.
BRIS-E'-IS	Captive assigned to Achilles as prize of honor and taken from him by Agamemnon.
CAL'-CHAS	Greek prophet. In the story of Troilus and Cressida Calchas is a Trojan who deserts to the Greeks.
CA-LYP'-SO	Nymph who kept Odysseus with her for many years on an island.
CAS-SAN'-DRA	Daughter of Priam. Trojan prophetess who was never believed.
CAS'-TOR	Brother of Helen.
CHA-RYB'-DIS	A whirlpool crossed by Odysseus on his travels.
CHIR'-ON	Old centaur who was tutor to Achilles and other heroes.
CHRY-SE'-IS	Daughter of Chryses and captive of Agamemnon.
CHRY'-SES	Priest of Apollo.
CLO'-NI-E	An Amazon.
CLY-TEM-NEST'-RA	Wife of Agamemnon and his murderess.
CO'-RAX	Place where the herdsmen of Odysseus fed his swine.

CO-ROEB'-US   Ally of the Trojans and affianced to Cas-
                     sandra.

CRES'-SID-A   Daughter of Calchas.

CRE-U'-SA   Wife of Aeneas lost in the taking of
                     Troy.

CYC'-NUS   Ally of the Trojans killed by Achilles.

DAWN GODDESS   Mother of Memnon, wife of Tithonus.

DE-I-DAM-I'-A   Wife of Achilles, mother of Pyrrhus.

DE-I'-PHO-BUS   A son of Priam and third husband of
                     Helen.

DE-ME'-TER   Goddess of the harvest.

DI'-O-MEDE   A Greek hero. Lover of Cressida and
                     companion of Odysseus on several ad-
                     ventures.

DIS'-CORD   The goddess who threw down the golden
                     apple.

DO'-LON   A spy sent out by Hector to investigate
                     doings in the Greek camp.

E-LYS'-I-UM   The dwelling place of the happy dead.

E-THI-O'-PI-A   Kingdom of Memnon, situated at the
                     eastern edge of the earth.

EU-MAE'-US   Faithful swineherd of Odysseus.

EU'-MEL-OS   A Greek hero, near-winner in the chariot
                     race.

EUR-Y'-MACH-US   Leader of Penelope's suitors.

EUR-Y'-PYL-US   Grandson of Heracles and ally of the
                     Trojans.

HA'-DES   Home of the dead.

HE'-BE   Goddess of youth.

HEC'-TOR   Son of Priam and chief Trojan hero.

HE'-CU-BA	Wife of Priam and queen of Troy.
HE'-LEN	Wife of Menelaus who eloped with Paris.
HE'-LEN-US	Son of Priam and a Trojan prophet.
HE-PHAIST'-OS	God of fire.
HER'-A	Queen of the gods and a chief supporter of the Greeks.
HER'-A-CLES	The strongest hero who ever lived.
HER'-MES	Messenger of Zeus.
HER-MI'-O-NE	Only child of Menelaus and Helen.
HY'-DRA	Poisonous serpent killed by Heracles.
I'-DA	Mountain behind Troy.
I-DAI'-OS	Servant of Priam.
I'-LUS	Grandfather of Priam, in memory of whom Troy was often called Ilium.
IPH-I-DAM'-AS	Son of Antenor killed by Agamemnon.
IPH-I-GEN-I'-A	Daughter of Agamemnon sacrificed by him to obtain a fair wind.
I'-RIS	Rainbow goddess.
I'-SOS	Son of Priam killed by Agamemnon.
I'-THA-CA	Island kingdom of Odysseus.
LA-ER'-TES	Father of Odysseus.
LA-O'-CO-ON	Trojan priest of Poseidon who was killed for attacking the Trojan horse.
LA-O-DAM-I'-A	Wife of Protesilaus who died of grief at his death.
LEI-O'-DES	One of Penelope's suitors.
LE'-TO	Mother of Apollo and Artemis.
LY-KA'-ON	Son of Priam who was twice caught by Achilles.

MA-CHA'-ON	A Greek hero skilled in medicine.
ME'-DON	Faithful servant of Telemachus.
ME-LAN'-THI-US	Goatherd and faithless servant of Odysseus.
MEM'-NON	King of Ethiopia and son of the goddess of dawn. Ally of the Trojans.
ME-NE-LA'-US	Brother of Agamemnon and husband of Helen.
MEN-IP'-PUS	A Greek hero killed by the Amazons.
MEN'-TOR	An old advisor of Telemachus whose form Athene assumed.
MER'-I-ON-ES	A Greek charioteer.
MY-CEN'-AE	Kingdom of Agamemnon.
MYR'-MID-ONS	People ruled over by Peleus and Achilles.
NAU'-PLI-US	Father of Palamedes who wrecked the returning Greeks in revenge for his son's death.
NES'-TOR	Oldest of the heroes.
O-DYS'-SEUS	Wisest of the heroes.
OE-NO'-NE	Nymph beloved by Paris before he met Helen.
OI'-LEUS	Father of the lesser Ajax.
O-LYMP'-US	Dwelling of the gods.
O-REST'-ES	Son of Agamemnon who avenged his father's murder by killing his mother.
PA-LA-MED'-ES	Crafty, ambitious hero who was put to death on a false charge of dealing with the Trojans.
PAL-LAD'-I-UM	Sacred image of Athene that stood on the citadel of Troy.
PAN'-DAR-US	Uncle of Cressida.

PAR'-IS	Son of Priam and seducer of Helen.
PA-TRO'-CLUS	Beloved friend of Achilles who was killed by Hector.
PE'-LEUS	Husband of Thetis and father of Achilles.
PE-NEL'-O-PE	Faithful wife of Odysseus.
PEN-THES-I-LE'-A	Amazon queen who came to help the Trojans and was killed by Achilles.
PHE'-MI-US	Minstrel in the hall of Odysseus.
PHIL-OC-TET'ES	Owner of the bow of Heracles who was abandoned on an island by the Greeks.
PILLARS OF HER'-A-CLES	Or Pillars of Hercules, now known as the Straits of Gibraltar.
PI-SIS'-TRAT-US	Youngest son of Nestor.
PO-DARC'-ES	Brother of Protesilaus.
PO-LIT'-ES	One of Priam's youngest sons.
POL'-LUX	Brother of Helen.
POL-Y'-DAM-AS	Trojan of the peace party and in opposition to Hector.
PO-LYX'-EN-A	Daughter of Priam sacrificed at the tomb of Achilles.
PO-SEI'-DON	God of the sea and friend of the Greeks.
PRI'-AM	King of Troy.
PRO-TES-I-LA'-US	First hero to land on the shore of Troy.
PRO'-TEUS	A wise sea god.
PY'-LOS	Kingdom of Nestor.
PYR'-RHUS	Son of Achilles.
RHE'-SUS	King of Thrace and ally of the Trojans, killed by Odysseus and Diomede.
SAL'-A-MIS	Island kingdom of Telamon, father of the greater Ajax.

SAR-PED'-ON	Son of Zeus. Ally of the Trojans.
SCY'-ROS	Island on which Achilles was concealed by his mother.
SI'-NON	Liar who persuaded the Trojans to accept the horse.
SKAI'-AN GATE	Gate of Troy leading to the plain.
SKA-MAN'-DER	River running by Troy.
SPAR'-TA	Kingdom of Menelaus.
STYX	River bordering the land of the dead.
TAL-THYB'-I-US	Herald of the Greeks.
TAUR'-IS	Land to which Artemis took Iphigenia.
TEC-MES'-SA	Slave of Ajax and mother of his son.
TE'-LA-MON	Father of Ajax and Teucer.
TE-LE'-MACH-US	Son of Odysseus.
TEU'-CER	Half-brother of Ajax and the son of a Trojan princess captured and enslaved by Telamon.
THE-AN'-O	Wife of Antenor and priestess of Athene.
THE'-BE	Native city of Andromache.
THE'-TIS	Sea goddess and mother of Achilles.
THRACE	Kingdom of Rhesus.
TI-THON'-US	Brother of Priam married to the goddess of dawn.
TROI'-LUS	Son of Priam and lover of Cressida.
TYN'-DAR-EUS	Father of Helen.
ZEUS	Father of gods and men.